THE EVOLUTION OF SPORTS SOCIAL MEDIA

BY AARON EISMAN

Charleston, SC
www.PalmettoPublishing.com

The Evolution of Sports Social Media

Paperback ISBN: 978-1-63837-146-5
Hardcover ISBN: 978-1-63837-147-2
eBook ISBN: 978-1-63837-148-9

To my Mom and Dad,
You both are meshuggeneh people, but I wouldn't have it any other way.
I am proud to be your son and love you both very much. XOXO

"Be a sponge. Spend as much time as possible with people who truly know their craft and be a great listener. That is how you learn.

- Jerry Colangelo

TABLE OF CONTENTS

INTRODUCTION

"Choose a job you love, and you will never have to
work a day in your life." —Confucius

I have been fortunate enough to work for three of the top sports companies
in the world: Turner Sports, Bleacher Report (B/R), and the NFL. First
off, I was part of the first social media team at Turner Sports in Atlanta,
Georgia. To work at a well-respected sports media outlet for one of my first
full-time positions out of college was an incredibly humbling experience.

As my time at Turner Sports progressed, I wanted to continue working
in sports social media. One of the managers at Turner Sports suggested I
check out Bleacher Report (Turner Sports is their parent company) and put
me in contact with their director of social media. Not too long after talking
to him, I had a job offer to move up to New York City. I joined B/R at the
perfect time. A few months after starting with the company, they saw the
opportunity in social media and hired numerous new employees for the
department. Little did I know at the time, that decision was one of the most
influential moves I made in my career.

After over two years with B/R I decided to move back home to Los
Angeles and work for the NFL. Another stop in my career that I'll never
forget. I participated in NFL Network's coverage of Super Bowl LIII by
posting the top highlights from our shows onto our social media accounts. I
couldn't have asked for a better experience in football, and to be back home
was the cherry on top.

Each of my experiences was different, and at every stop in my career, I consumed as much knowledge as possible. My mom told me to be a sponge and soak up the knowledge in my work environments, and that advice led me to success at each company I have been at. Whether it was Turner Sports, Bleacher Report, or the NFL, I cherished the opportunity I was given and never took it for granted.

I've worked at many big companies covering all kinds of events and posting their highlights for social media branding, from Turner Sports' coverage of the 2015 NBA Finals to taking charge of the NFL Network's social media for Super Bowl LIII. But the company that started all of that for me was Bleacher Report. When I got there, we had roughly seven hundred thousand followers on Instagram. Now, the company is on their way to hitting seventeen million followers this year.

Before it turned into the Bleacher Report it is today, I joined the company when we had only four other people on the social media team: a director of social media and three others who had a similar sports media background to myself. There were changes that turned Bleacher Report into a social media-focused company later in 2015, just months after I arrived. The social media team went from five people to over twenty people within a six-month period.

Did other sports social media teams catch up? They did by hiring more people in the next few years, but B/R set the gold standard. But sports social media and my book is not just about Bleacher Report. It's about the industry as a whole. Nowadays, every sports team and media company and most sports agencies have at least one person dedicated solely to social media.

The size of the sports industry is enormous! There are over one hundred professional teams, more than twenty major sports media outlets, and thousands upon thousands of professional athletes that are managed by over three hundred sports agencies. With that comes millions of sports social media posts per week. With all that competition, you stand out by creating the best content. My firm belief is that "content is king," especially in this day and age. Creating viral moments is harder than it seems. You need to create content that literally stops the scroll of the user and get them to engage with it. With all of the content and platforms these days, it's easier said than done.

With all the competition, the publishers in sports social media are posting to attract the consumption of the audience and get those people to engage with the post, or an extra follow can't hurt either. Your content needs to stand out compared to other social media accounts so that your posts work with that platform's algorithm to increase your chances of getting seen by more eyeballs.

We are all fighting over the time of the audience spends looking at your post and the way they engage with it. Understanding the consumption habits of the audience in each generation is the key to success. But platforms change, algorithms change, and the consumptions habits of each generation can change overnight. So each sports social media team needs to be really nimble over time.

At the end of the day, as one of my mentors told me, "Sports social media is more than just a bunch of twenty-year-olds tweeting." There's a lot behind the scenes that the audience doesn't see. These days, social media duties include brand analysis/brand loyalty, strategy, content creation (photography, videography, and graphic design), posting, monetization, analytics, and more duties to the job. There's a method to the madness. Maybe not an exact science because of the ever-changing nature of the industry, but a job in social media is not easy these days.

In a study in October 2020, 4.14 billion people around the world are using social media (53% of Earth's population).[1] With tons of viral posts each day, everybody and their dog thinks they can manage a social media account. That couldn't be farther from the truth. Social media management is a science unto itself, and the process for creating content for a multibillion-dollar industry is far more involved than the average social media account for your cat.

Creating great content is a must in engaging the audience these days. LeBron James didn't create Taco Tuesday, but he did champion the phrase. He posted a video starting this tradition on his Instagram story. An example of how this moment took off was when House Highlights' YouTube channel posted his first Taco Tuesday video, and it got over two million views and forty thousand likes. That's not even including numerous accounts posting this clip on Instagram, Facebook, Twitter, Snapchat, etc. His Taco Tuesday videos have generated over ten million views and over one million interactions.[2] The power of sports social media!

Personally, I am fascinated with why a superstar athlete talking about food gets this much attention. I wrote this book because I am fascinated with moments like these and because the knowledge of what goes into creating an 80 million-follower social media account with viral posts every week is lacking.

I am compelled to write this book because sports social media has a special place in my heart. I've had a career that I didn't know I would have had in 2013, thanks to the increase of jobs in the industry. There is a lack of knowledge when it comes to the audience with how complex a sports social media team is these days. There are a social editor/manager or multiple people (who do the posting), a graphic designer, a video editor, an analytics expert, a social sales team, and others that create a robust team.

After graduating from Indiana University in 2013, I wasn't sure where my journalism degree could take me. You couldn't major in social media when I entered college in 2009. That's when my journey into the world of digital content began: at the beginnings of social media. Since 2013 I've had eight years of experience working at major sports businesses and creating countless viral content. I've watched this career path grow and have grown with it, something that gives me a unique perspective on the development and iteration of the sports social media landscape. This wasn't the career I envisioned coming into college, but this was the career that chose me in 2013.

Over the past eight years, I have had the pleasure of learning from some of the top people in sports social media. From Morgan Dewan (the first director of social media at Turner Sports) to the Malamut brothers (the creators of Game of Zones) to Omar Raja (the founder of House of Highlights). I used that sponge mentality and consumed as much knowledge as possible. Whether it was Turner Sports, Bleacher Report, or the NFL, I always had room to grow and new people to learn from. I'm happy to say that I've chosen a career that I have fallen in love with.

The biggest piece of information I learned? Staying ahead of the social media game means creating "thumb-stopping content," content that literally makes someone stop scrolling through their news feed to engage with the post.

Thumb-stopping content is more relevant today than ever because there's so much competition in the news feed. Before, you would follow high-level brands that matter to you, but now anyone's post can go viral because of how the algorithm has changed. If you can create "thumb-stopping content" and stop the scroll of someone's news feed, you have gold in today's world. But doing that is harder than it seems.

Making a viral post back in the day for Bleacher Report wasn't easy, and it's tougher these days. It's not easy because original content (content produced by the company, team, or athlete) doesn't always connect with the audience, even after you've spent days or even weeks on ideation and execution of the post. This book will help you understand how that thumb-stopping content is made.

This book takes an in-depth look into the birth of the sports social media industry in 2009–10, when B/R changed the game in 2016–2018, how content going viral is tougher than ever today, and where things are headed in the future. I can't say it enough, but sports social media is complex because of all the different types of people it takes to be successful. From editors to creatives to analysts to marketing and more. If you want to learn about why sports social media is more advanced than any other social media category, then this is the book for you. Sports social media is a combination of marketing, public relations, content creation, sales, and other departments in an organization. It means everything to every person in sports because it's the voice of a company. Being the voice of a company allows you to connect with another person because you represent that company.

Whether you're a social media professional, a social media student in college, or a sports fan, this is the book for you because you will learn the power of sports social media and the impact it has on millions of people around the world.

When it comes to the wide world of sports, an industry with millions being poured into media content, time means money. This book will show you how that landscape is navigated, from conception to now, and give you valuable insight into why content is king. You'll also learn why strategy is vital for success and how sports social media has turned into a multi-million-dollar field in just ten years.

So get ready to be the sponge that my mom taught me to be and to fully understand why every sports company needs more than just one intern running the show. There's a lot more to the sports social media world than you can't even fathom. This book will go into every inch of sports social media and what it takes to be successful through the years.

Fasten your seatbelt and let's get started!

NOTES:

1. "Social Media Users—Datareportal–Global Digital Insights." 2020. *Datareportal—Global Digital Insights.* https://datareportal.com/social-media-users.

2. Sourced via CrowdTangle Research over posts that use Taco Tuesday referring to LeBron James.

CHAPTER 1:

DOWN GOES SHAQ! WHAT LED TO MY FIRST VIRAL POST

"Down goes Shaq!"

These three words may make no sense to you, but they are the reason why I love sports social media. I've used these words twice in my career. Both times they led to viral posts for the NBA on TNT's social media accounts. These were two of my top posts during my work at Turner Sports.

I'm no wordsmith or Shakespeare of my time, but I learned quickly in the industry of sports social media that simplicity is key. Those words I chose couldn't be more basic, but they did a great job of setting up the video where Shaq went down.

Sadly, I can't get the exact numbers on those two posts; Facebook and Twitter didn't record video views in 2014. But from what I gathered, those posts accumulated over one hundred thousand engagements (likes, comments, and shares) on Facebook, ten thousand engagements (retweets, favorites, and replies) on Twitter, over four million Vine loops (rest in peace), and almost two million views on YouTube.[1]

These numbers weren't my best posts ever, but they are two that I will always remember because the account I managed went viral. This was at the very early stage of my sports social media career, and I was watching TNT's Inside the NBA, waiting for a social media worthy clip. These two scenes that popped up were the perfect opportunities to engage NBA fans all around the world. All it took was grabbing the clip using SnappyTV (a former live TV clipping service now owned by Twitter), downloading the video, and pressing send on all the platforms we had accounts on. Before I knew it, those clips were getting thousands of engagements, video views, and shares from the NBA audience. That feeling when you see a post take off is like getting an instant injection of dopamine; it's really tough to describe unless you've gone viral before.

"There is that dopamine hit. I don't want to sound like I live my life off of likes and retweets, but I imagine it's like many drugs, and the high is similar to the dopamine hit that you get when you see your content taking off," Timberwolves social media manager Cody Sharrett said.[2]

Another person in sports social media shared the same sentiment. And I couldn't agree more.

"There is such a rush with creating something that did well, that quote unquote went viral or did a lot better than normal. That feeling is probably a little bit addictive, it's kind of like a drug," an NBA social media director said.[3]

Those first few times when posts like "Down goes Shaq!" went viral meant a lot to me. I experienced instant gratification because of the numbers. A pat on the back from my fellow team members. A screenshot of the post going on my parent's fridge. It's hard to explain unless you've gone viral in the past. Moments like these create lasting happy memories for the person who pushed the send button.

In sports social media, you have to work for a social media account with media rights, be in the right place to capture the moment, and use a strong voice and engaging caption to gain the audience's attention. Being in the right place at the right time sounds cliché, but it's true. Going viral doesn't happen often because there is so much competition with similar sports social media accounts, but when it does it's truly memorable for the person who posted it.

HOW DID I LAND THE TURNER SPORTS JOB?

Over the years, people have asked me how I worked at such well-respected sports brands like Turner Sports, Bleacher Report, and the NFL. I usually say persistence, hard work, and creativity have helped me along the way, and they are truly what helped "keep me in the doors" at these companies. My story of getting to Turner Sports to launch my sports social media career did not take the traditional route.

I grew up loving sports and believing I was going to be the Jewish Larry Bird one day. I adored basketball. Watching it, playing it, and talking about it with my friends and family. But instead of being like "The Hick from French Lick" (Bird's nickname), I was more like the mensch on the bench. Dictionary definition of mensch is a person of integrity and honor.[4]

I loved basketball and wanted to play in the NBA one day, but sadly I learned early that dream would not come to fruition. I'm 5'10" and not very athletic. Also, as my brother told me, "There's like a 0.00000000001% chance of making the NBA." Not the exact number he used, but you get the point.

My dreams were crushed. But like many people who love sports and don't play collegiately or professionally, I wanted to have a career in the sports industry (not the easiest route either). There is a ton of competition because of all the people that don't make it professionally might turn to working in sports. So what's next for this sports fanatic from Los Angeles? Find a way to get a career in sports.

I had a passion for journalism at a young age. Starting around twelve or thirteen, I would go down the driveway every morning to pick up the *Los Angeles Times* and read the sports section. Also, I watched a ton of sports television growing up. Sitting next to my brother and dad, we would watch Vin Scully call Dodgers games, Broncos legend John Elway—my all-time favorite QB—throw touchdown passes to Shannon Sharpe, and USC vs. UCLA football games. I consumed as much as I could.

After realizing my dream of playing sports professionally was over, I began a new dream: become a sportswriter at the *Los Angeles Times*. How do you get to the *LA Times*? Get a journalism degree. In 2009, I applied to colleges all over the country looking for the best institution to give me a good print journalism background.

After mulling over the schools I was accepted to, I decided to attend Indiana University (IU). They had one of the top college newspapers, *Indiana Daily Student (IDS),* and a very good sports radio station called WIUX. I packed my bags and moved to Bloomington, Indiana where I would spend the next four years.

I'll always remember the moment I got a Twitter account. In August 2009, I was a freshman at IU and was in Telecommunications 101 with more than four hundred other students. The professor of the course asked the auditorium of students to raise our hands if we had a Twitter account. Out of the entire class, fewer than thirty students raised their hands. He then said to us, "You all need to get a Twitter account today. It's the future of social media. It's micro-blogging." So during that extremely humid day in August, I got my Twitter account. I didn't know it then, but that day is still a vivid memory.

I didn't do any live tweeting of any sporting events until a year or two later. As the world continued to go more digital, I started tweeting more on that Twitter account. In 2004, fewer than one million people were on MySpace; Facebook had not even launched. By 2018, Facebook had more 2.26 billion users with other sites also growing to hundreds of millions of users. Social media is the epitome of how the world was slowly changing in the late 2000s.[5]

Other forms of technology became important for my life before social media helped me professionally. In 2010, I started to write blogs for the teams I was covering for the student newspaper. They incentivized blog writing by paying us five dollars per blog. Major proof that the world was becoming more digital was the ability to hear my live radio broadcasts anywhere in the world. Crazy, right? At the time, it was revolutionary. I don't remember what year that changed, but it allowed my family in Los Angeles to listen to the sports games I broadcasted in the Midwest.

From 2009–2013, I saw numerous changes in how we were starting to use digital and slowly going away from print journalism. This scared me because at the time I thought I was going to be a sportswriter for the *Los*

Angeles Times coming out of college. So after graduating in May 2013, I came to a crossroads in my career path: take the traditional print journalism route and work for a small-town newspaper to get started in the business or look for digital sports jobs.

After applying all over the country, I accepted my first job with a startup named Movoli (which later changed its name to SPORTalk) in New York City. Movoli was a sports social media platform that would allow fans from around the world the opportunity to interact via a game wall. Sadly, my job didn't last too long. The startup started to go downhill after six months, and I decided to leave.

My thought process was to get another job in New York City with a big media company where I could establish some roots and start to build my network. I applied all over NYC hoping to stay there, but I saw an intriguing job post on my Indeed profile: "T3 Social Media Editor at Turner Sports in Atlanta, Georgia." I decided to apply because Atlanta was a big city, Turner Sports is a great sports media company, and I needed to pay off my college loans.

I interviewed with three people in the organization then got a call a week later saying that I should look for an email from human resources with my job offer. That got me out of the funk I was in due to the failure of my first job out of college. I learned later from a manager on the social media team that over nine thousand people applied for nine positions with Turner Sports. I accepted the job offer, signed the contract, and booked a flight just two weeks later. In October 2014, I packed my two bags and moved down to Atlanta for a new adventure.

MORGAN DEWAN'S APPROACH TO BUILDING A SOCIAL MEDIA TEAM IN 2014

After graduating from Duke University, Morgan Dewan (my future boss and mentor) worked in publicity, brand marketing, and advertising for JCPenney, H-E-B Grocery Company, AT&T, and other Fortune 500 companies. She spent eight years working for these companies until accepting a position with Turner Sports as the director of social media in February 2013. The media conglomerate made a major decision by hiring a social media-focused employee, a very groundbreaking move by former Turner Sports President Lenny Daniels. Social media in sports was still in its infancy, but Turner Sports made a decision to ramp up social media coverage.

"Turner Sports called and said, 'Look, we're looking to build a social media practice here. Would you be interested in coming over?'" Dewan said.

Dewan became the face of Turner Sports social media, but building a team in 2013–2014 wasn't easy. As she said in the Brand Story Inc. podcast, it takes buy-in from senior management. "The first step, what I gave to Turner Sports, was really justifying why we needed to put a dedicated team towards it, that it really was a service for the entire organization. And that's how I presented it." Dewan said.[6]

Dewan hired a few more people full-time before making the major move to hire a team of nine recent college grads to train and run Turner Sports social media and its properties. Just like Dewan said, other Turner Sports employees saw the same struggle to build a social media team in 2014.

In October 2014, nine recent college graduates and myself included were hired to run social media for Turner Sports as part of the Turner Trainee Team (T3) program.

Why were we chosen instead of people with more experience in the social media industry?

"A lot of the reason that we were able to get the funding of what we needed is because we knew that we could attract and retain and grow young people who are endemic to the social media space," Dewan said on the Brand Story Inc. podcast.[6]

This was the basis of social media education for my career. People like Dewan and others allowed us millennials to be the 24/7 team to run social media accounts like NBA TV, NBA on TNT, March Madness (during the tournament), and PGA.com.

Our team was diverse in our skill sets, but we all grew up with social media and had an existing knowledge of how to use it. The team was composed of two other social media editors and two graphic designers, three analytics employees, and one ideation specialist. At times, we were called "super interns," but we had a major impact on social media for Turner Sports.

Those Shaq posts that I mentioned earlier are two of the most memorable posts in my eight-year career in sports social media, but the one on Christmas was particularly special. Let me set the stage for how the day went down. I was in Los Angeles visiting my family during the holidays. It was perfect timing to get away from Atlanta, where it was forty-some degrees and close to snowing. It was seventy-two degrees and sunny in LA, and I was covering sports from my home (living the dream). My dad set up a makeshift desk in front of the TV. My parents ordered Chinese food (our Jewish Christmas tradition) which was placed next to my laptop.

We turned on TNT to watch the game, and I had open numerous tabs on my browser including Spredfast (our social media scheduling tool) and SnappyTV. While we watched the *Inside the NBA* halftime show and I ate my orange chicken, I saw Shaq fall into the Christmas tree. At that moment, I knew I had social media gold. I quickly edited the video on SnappyTV and downloaded the video to my phone. I then published the video out on Vine, then Twitter, then Facebook with the caption "Down goes Shaq!" This was before NBA on TNT's social media had an Instagram account. The numbers were phenomenal for the time, turning into not just the top sports social media post of the day, but also the month, and maybe the year. The post went viral, and I got recognition from my manager, Morgan, and the rest of the team, which was super gratifying.

For the eleven months of my contract, I published over 11,500 pieces of content across Facebook, Twitter, Instagram (IG), and Vine, which accumulated over 210 million total engagements and over 150 million video views. These numbers sound crazy, but I did the math (thanks to CrowdTangle Analytics tool).[1]

We did some amazing things at Turner Sports. We launched the IG accounts for those two properties as well. We did all of this in an eleven-month span. Our team would go over strategy for major tentpole events like NBA Opening Day, March Madness, and the PGA Championship. We also broke down the analytics and held other team meetings where we could get out our creative ideas and find ways to help the overall team.[1]

All these moments launched the beginning of my sports social media career. Social media is obviously more than just going viral. But you will always remember those first viral posts of your career. So thanks to Shaq for his clumsiness or good acting or whatever you want to call it.

But the biggest moment started with me being at the right place at the right time to capture a perfect moment on the *Inside the NBA* show. I thought I was going to be a sportswriter, but my journey turned left onto the path of sports social media. This was over twenty years in the making, but I'm glad I ended up where I did: sitting down, eating Chinese food, watching my favorite sports show on Christmas, and covering the broadcast for the social media team.

Shaq will never know the affect he had on my career, but I'm happy to call him a former coworker of mine. The thrill of going viral with those two posts was more than just a dopamine hit; it was a career-changer. "Down goes Shaq!" grew my love for sports social media and changed my career trajectory forever.

Thanks, big guy.

CITATIONS:

1. Source found through research of CrowdTangle and Facebook analytics.

2. Cody Sharrett, phone call with author, November 9, 2020.

3. Anonymous NBA social media director, phone call with author, December 17, 2020.

4. *Merriam-Webster*, s.v. "mensch (*n.*)," 2021, https://www.merriam-webster.com/dictionary/mensch.

5. Madeleine Hillyer, "Here's How Technology Has Changed The World Since 2000," *World Economic Forum*, 2018, https://www.weforum.org/agenda/2020/11/

heres-how-technology-has-changed-and-changed-us-over-the-past-20-years/.

6. Jay Sharman. "Turner Sports—Morgan Dewan." *Brand Story Inc.,* May 5, 2020, Podcast, MP3 audio.

7. Neelam Mulchandani, phone call with author, December 3, 2020.

CHAPTER 2:

HOW DID SPORTS SOCIAL MEDIA GET HERE?

What was the beginning of sports social media?

Before we get into the nitty-gritty of sports social media, we need to talk about when social media started. The first two social media platforms were Six Degrees and Friendster.[1] There's a good chance you've never heard of either. Out of my ninety-plus interviews for this book, only one person heard of Friendster, and no one knew what Six Degrees was.

"It was very basic. I would say, you just kind of connected to people. Maybe there was a chat version built in. I can't even remember, but I used it mostly to post pictures and share them with the group that I was connected to," Neelam Mulchandani said about Friendster.[2]

Six Degrees officially launched in 1997, and it lasted until about 2001. It's number of users peaked at around 3.5 million[1]. In 2002, the site Friendster emerged[1] A few months after its launch, Friendster had over three million users, and this number continued to grow, eventually reaching over one hundred million. In 2015, it suspended all of its services, and on Jan 1, 2019, it ceased all operations and officially closed its doors. The fact that Friendster had over one hundred million people on the social media platform, but only one person from my interviews heard of it is pretty astonishing.[1]

Right after Six Degrees and Friendster launched, other platforms that my interviewees have heard of were started. LinkedIn was founded in 2002, MySpace in 2003, Facebook or The Facebook in 2004, YouTube in 2005, Twitter in 2006, Instagram in 2010, and Snapchat in 2011[1].

I was actually very fond of MySpace and AOL Instant Messenger (AIM) before sophomore year of high school in 2006. My AIM username was HoopstarASE. I know, embarrassing, right? But I was huge NBA fan, and I thought I would be the Jewish Larry Bird one day (because of the blond hair and my solid three-point shooting).

Dewan vividly remembers when Facebook first touched her life. She was a junior at Duke in 2004. "When Facebook began, it rolled out at Harvard first, and then it went to all of the Ivy League schools. And so I had some friends who were attending Ivy League schools who were telling us that this was the new craze. Immediately after Facebook expanded to the Ivy League schools, they added Stanford to Duke, so we were really one of the first schools that had Facebook," she said.

Two years later, things changed when Facebook allowed anyone claiming to be above the age of thirteen to be on the platform.[3] This allowed in a new and younger demographic, and their user base changed forever. According to a *New York Times* article in 2006, "The move is meant to help the site expand, but it risks undercutting one of its attractions: it has been more exclusive and somewhat more protected than MySpace, its larger and more freewheeling rival."[4] A mix of expanding Facebook's audience, while trying to defeat rival MySpace. "If we make it so other young people can use the site, it strengthens the experience for everybody," Facebook founder Mark Zuckerberg said in that NY Times article.[4] In 2007, a year after Facebook expanded its age range, I was a junior in high school, and I got a Facebook page.

The two main elements of Facebook were the profile and the network. Each profile was linked to an individual person, and it was visible to all users of Facebook if permitted by privacy settings. It may include information such as contact information, whether you are in a relationship, your political views, your favorite music, books, and films, information about where you study, and a photo.[3]

I remember it was a place to connect with friends, write text status updates, and show all of your interests and hobbies. A lot of people really used Facebook as an educational tool to get to know people, to find out which people had the same friends as you, liked the same movies, or were in a relationship or not. I remember the relationship status being a big deal back in high school. Once you got into college, you would profile-stalk your future roommate, people in the same dorm, and other people with similar interests.

It's funny to see that while Facebook was such a big part of my life from 2007–2017, now I spend more of my time on Instagram, Twitter, and TikTok. Once most young people's parents, grandparents, and other extended family members got an account, Facebook stopped being so cool. We found new shiny toys and went to other platforms. Who knows which platforms will have my attention next year?

During my freshman year of college in August 2009, I got my Twitter account. I've done over thirteen thousand tweets since launching my account. It wasn't easy to do a 140-character tweet at the time, but it grew on me over the years.

THE DISRUPTIVE VOICE OF THE LOS ANGELES KINGS TWITTER ACCOUNT

Twitter didn't make a major impact on sports until the early 2010s. During my research and interviews, a number of people mentioned the Los Angeles Kings social media account run by Pat Donahue and Dewayne Hankins from 2010–2012 and how their team slowly started to change the sports social media industry. In 2012, Deadspin (rest in peace) even named an article "The Spunky Genius of Twitter's @LAKings." Deadspin was a sports blog founded by Will Leitchin 2005 and based in Chicago.[5]

It all started with Hankins sitting down with Kings leadership for a job interview asking them to buy into the idea that social media could be fun, and the team could have a unique voice to engage the audience. Hankins was working for another NHL team at the time, the Minnesota Wild, before joining the Kings.

"I sat down with the president of business operations, Luc Robitaille, and COO Chris McGowan, and I remember telling them all these ideas that I had with the Minnesota Wild. They were super excited about doing these things, and they wanted to be different. They wanted the marketing team to own the social accounts, and that got me super excited," former director of digital media Hankins said.[6]

Hankins and Donahue wanted to be different than all of the other NHL teams because social media could engage fans.

"We could be doing things in the game that would get our fans excited. I don't think any teams had any luck really pushing their team presidents, leaders, or executives to do, and it was a lot because they didn't know what social media was. They didn't know what the platforms were, and they didn't really want to do anything. They didn't really want to push the envelope," Hankins said.[6]

It was more of the Kings social media trying to write jokes and experiment where the line was back in 2010. Donahue and Hankins tested the line to see the response from leadership and find ways to work together.

"There wasn't even a long leash. I don't know if there was a leash, and it was like, cool, I'm going to write jokes, we're going to go for this and really kind of like push this to find where the line was because there was no line," Donahue said.[7]

During the 2012 Stanley Cup Finals, the Kings account tweeted banter at the New Jersey Devils by saying, "Aside from fist pumping, what else is there do in NJ?" The tweet refers to a dance move on the popular show *Jersey Shore*. This tweet clearly shows their personality of the Kings while not crossing the line. The Kings ended up winning the franchise's first championship that year. The Kings were one of the game changers in the early days of sports social media.

"In a lot of ways, we were the only team that was allowed to be that way, and we knew that by ribbing teams a little bit, it would force them to respond or not respond," Hankins said.[6] "The LA Kings account's personality was just our personality. At the end of the day, it was just Pat and I, and we have very similar sense of humor, so it worked out."

"From a social perspective, we're going to add personality to the brand, which in 2020 seems like so simple, but in 2010, that was not something that teams did. Teams didn't tell jokes. Teams didn't talk to fans. Teams didn't have any personality. It was like press releases and photographs was kind of where we were," Donahue said.[7]

Praise came from Deadspin because of the way the Kings' voice differentiated itself from all of the other teams in professional sports.

"But where the Kings' hockey triumph has followed a traditional path—talented young team with otherworldly goalie changes coaches, acquires another sniper, wins in postseason—their Twitter voice is something new. It's servicey, yes, but also puerile and deadpan. There's personality in the Kings' stream. The subscriber knows there's a human sensibility behind the feed and appreciates it," writer Jack Dickey said in the Deadspin article.[8]

The same sentiment rang true with sports fans and sports social media professionals around the country. The Kings were the first team to use voice to their advantage.

"I always tip my cap to the LA Kings of the early 2010s. Pro sports team I can think of that was taking shots at their opponents and just using Twitter in a very different way," said senior director, content strategy at the Washington Football Team Rael Enteen.[9]

Current LA Kings social media manager Katlyn Gambill remembers the Kings had a different voice on social media compared to other sports teams: "I remember being so annoyed with the Kings Twitter account. They were just so darn good at it. They were so good at being snarky and grabbing people that didn't care about hockey. They really laid out the entire landscape for sports social media marketing and having personality, and it doesn't have to just be a photo of a player skating. They really did a great job of making sure that they were the first ones to kind of define everything."[10]

The Kings showed attitude with their voice and were pioneers in the sports social media space. Compared to other social media platforms, Twitter is a great place to showcase your unique voice. Before Twitter allowed the use of pictures and video, all you had was 140 characters and voice to hook a reader's attention. A common theme between the LA Kings and Turner

Sports was having leadership to buy into the idea of having personality with a certain voice or hiring numerous people to develop a team.

"I think what happened was we were lucky enough to have leaders at the company who believed in the future of social and believed that engagement was the key. In order to have engagement, you needed to have personality," Hankins said.[5]

THE BIRTH OF TURNER SPORTS SOCIAL MEDIA

Two years after the LA Kings made their mark on the industry, I believe Turner Sports built the biggest sports social media team. Turner Sports wasn't the first, but they grew into one of the largest in 2014. ESPN had a social production team that would do TV production and social media, but Turner Sports hired full-time social media staff to run their property accounts. Maybe I'm a little biased since I worked there from October 2014 to September 2015.

I can talk from personal experience that Turner Sports was innovative at the time. Former Turner Sports President Lenny Daniels hired Morgan Dewan as the director of social media in February of 2013. The decision to hire a social media-focused employee was groundbreaking, but it was also a gamble. Having a social media team cost money, and there was no historical evidence to suggest it would pay off.

After that move, Dewan said it took time to be able to convince the higher-ups to hire a full social media team.

"At that moment in 2013, I didn't see the ability to build a forty- or fifty-person team out of the gate. I knew that I would be kind of ridiculed for trying to do that. But what I did see was that we can approach it in three different ways. We can build a team that is in direct reflection of the marketing, digital, content, and revenue goals that we have, as part of the organization. So that's what we did, we set up a team that was all around social content," Dewan said on the Brand Story Inc. podcast.[12]

Dewan got the green light to launch the social media team. I do know that Turner Sports was one of the first sports social media teams to hire more than a few people to run major accounts (three hundred thousand-plus followers). Over the next year, Morgan had to figure out Turner Sports' hiring plan to help manage properties like NBA on TNT, NBA TV, March Madness, PGA.com, and others.

This is where I come in. I was applying to digital, social, writing, and all kinds of sports jobs all around the country. After interviewing with over thirty companies in a four-month span, I interviewed with Morgan and landed my first sports social media job. Unemployment was over.

Morgan and other higher-ups gave us the opportunity to really flex our muscles at an early stage of all of our careers.

The purpose of our team was to grab all of the content from the many properties and post them on our Facebook, Twitter, and Vine accounts. NBA on TNT and NBA TV didn't get an Instagram account until mid-2015 (halfway into my eleven-month contract). "Our only job was really capturing the content that was already living around the building. It was going down to the coordinating producer of NBA TV and saying, 'Hey, what's hitting your cutting room floor? Can I use that?' So we were really scrappy in the beginning," Dewan said on the Brand Story Inc. podcast.[12]

Members of our T3 team were the ones posting, ideating, analyzing, and coming up with the daily creative execution for properties like NBA on TNT, NBA TV, March Madness (during the tournament), and PGA.com.

Together the entire social media team truly accomplished some amazing things during my time there. Our team was innovative, creative, and disruptive in the sports social media industry. This was the formative experience in my sports social media career. I could not be more grateful to Morgan, Neelam, and the other higher-ups that gave our social media team a chance.

As Dewan said in the Brand Story Inc. podcast, "Content was dripping off the walls of this place."[12] Our social media team consumed all of the content, posted it on various platforms, and the results were astonishing. We were the first social media team at Turner Sports.

The common theme between the Kings and Turner Sports is the buy-in from higher-ups. People like Kings president of business operations Luc Robitaille and COO Chris McGowan allowed Donahue and Hankins to flex their voice on social media and test the line. For Turner Sports, President Lenny Daniels allowed Dewan to grow the social media team with young millennials. Both decisions proved to be impactful for the sports social media industry.

At the end of my Turner Sports contract, I knew it was only the beginning of the golden era of sports social media. Bleacher Report (my next position) would revolutionize the industry in 2015–2018.

CITATIONS:

1. Matthew Jones, "The Complete History Of Social Media: A Timeline Of The Invention Of Online Networking," History Cooperative, 2015, https://historycooperative.org/the-history-of-social-media/.

2. Neelam Mulchandani, phone call with author, December 3, 2020.

3. Niels Brügger, "A Brief History Of Facebook As A Media Text: The Development Of An Empty Structure," First Monday, 2015.

4. Saul Hansell, "Site Previously For Students Will Be Opened To Others," The New York Times, September 12, 2006, Technology, https://www.nytimes.com/2006/09/12/technology/12online.html.

5. Wikipedia; Wikipedia's "Deadspin" entry; Accessed January 18, 2021. https://en.wikipedia.org/wiki/Deadspin.

6. Dewayne Hankins, phone call with author, January 15, 2021.

7. Pat Donahue, phone call with author, January 8, 2021.

8. Jack Dickey, "The Spunky Genius Of Twitter's @Lakings, The Second-Biggest Surprise Of The Playoffs," Deadspin, 2020. https://deadspin.com/the-spunky-genius-of-twitters-lakings-the-second-bigg-5910962.

9. Rael Enteen, phone call with author, December 3, 2020.

10. Katlyn Gambill, phone call with author, December 7, 2020.

11. Morgan Dewan, phone call with author, November 3, 2020.

12. Sharman, Jay. "Turner Sports—Morgan Dewan." Brand Story Inc., May 5, 2020. Podcast, MP3 audio.

CHAPTER 3:

THE BIRTH OF SOCIAL MEDIA AT ESPN

"You have to know the past to understand the present," —American astronomer Carl Sagan[1]

Entertainment and Sports Programming Network. You might not know the full name, but you know the acronym, ESPN. I didn't know what ESPN's acronym stood for until I looked on Wikipedia. ESPN has always been in my life, as it has for anyone that loves sports. Their slogan is literally "The worldwide leader in sports."[2]

ESPN was started on September 7, 1979. They launched the show SportsCenter that same day, which averages up to 115 million viewers per month.[3] From that day on when ESPN launched, the sports world changed forever. You should know the history of ESPN because they have always been a big part of my life and the sports social media world too. I didn't work there, but I always respected "the mothership," as one of my Indiana University professors called them.

Growing up, ESPN had some of my favorite shows on TV. From *SportsCenter* to *Pardon the Interruption (PTI)* to *Around the Horn (ATH)* to *First Take*. They were a part of my daily routine. I would start my day off by reading the Los Angeles Times sports section. Then my dad would drive me to school, and we would listen to the radio station 710 ESPN-AM. Every morning from middle school to high school, we would hear Colin Cowherd talk about all things sports. Although school was only a ten-minute drive, my dad and I would bond over our passion for sports.

I would get home from school around three-ish and immediately turn on ESPN. First, I would watch *Around the Horn (ATH)* and felt a bond with host Tony Reali, even though we didn't know each other. Also, watching sports writers on the show got me excited because I wanted to be them growing up. Sportswriters like Bill Plaschke (Los Angeles Times), Woody Paige (The Gazette), and J.A. Adande (former LA Times) I admired because of their knowledge of sports and wise opinions on current events. Those were some of the reasons why I wanted to become a sportswriter growing up. Not the most sought-after career in middle school.

Each episode, four sports writers would banter over national sports topics and earn points with who made a better argument. After ATH finished each day, I would leave on ESPN to watch Pardon the Interruption featuring Tony Kornheiser and Michael Wilbon. The show has been running since 2001, and I've been watching it since at least 2005. Both Kornheiser and Wilbon have infectious personalities and tremendous sports knowledge, explaining why the show has been running for twenty years.

THE BATTLE OF THE GIANTS

I graduated from Indiana University with a journalism degree in 2013 hoping to work at ESPN one day. Do I want to live in Bristol, Connecticut (ESPN's headquarters)? Not really, but to work for ESPN in the future would be an honor. Although I have yet to work at "the worldwide leader in sports," ESPN has always been a competitor in the eyes of my past companies.

During my time at Turner Sports, we competed with ESPN in the NBA world. Both companies have owned NBA television rights for years. In 2014, the NBA announced a new nine-year television deal that would begin the 2016–17 season and last through 2024–25 for both companies. The deal is reportedly worth $2.6 or $2.7 billion per year.[5] This is a massive deal in sports television rights, and the number will only go up in the next contract. As viewership and inflation increases, so does the cost for NBA television rights.

I helped manage the NBA TV and NBA on TNT social media accounts along with two other editors. Daily through a nine-month season, the three of us would post constantly on Facebook, Twitter, and Vine (Instagram wasn't relevant for Turner Sports until 2015). There was always one editor on from 9:00 a.m.–5:00 p.m. for daily news and another one on from 4:00 p.m.–2:00 a.m. covering games and TV shows on our channels.

Every week featured a bunch of games either on ESPN, NBA on TNT, NBA TV, or local broadcast stations. At Turner Sports, we were allowed to clip and edit any games because of the billions the company was paying for these rights. Each game night could feature ten to fifteen clips from the various games on these networks. At one point, there became competitiveness between Turner and ESPN.

Mainly the conflict started because there were no discussions of digital/social media rights in the contract before the 2014 announcement. It wasn't as important as it turned into when 2013–2014 rolled around. That was truly the start of NBA highlights being posted on social media. There were no guidelines as to which media companies could post which highlights. We had free rein to do as we pleased. At one point, ESPN reached out to my boss Dewan to tell her that Turner Sports wasn't allowed to post NBA highlights from Christmas games on their network.

This was a big deal because before that, we could post any ESPN highlights to our social media channels. There was no restriction. But Christmas is a very big deal in the NBA. Usually there are four or five games, and they are all nationally televised because of the importance of the day. Thanksgiving games to the NFL are like Christmas games to the NBA. ESPN's decision caused strife with a few members of our social media team. Why would they make this decision a day before Christmas? Is it because we're competitors or they just wanted to sole purpose of posting their owned content?

This was not the last time one of the companies I had worked for had this competitiveness with ESPN. While I was at Bleacher Report, there were numerous times where we felt the unspoken tension between the two companies. Social media is a very competitive business between sports media companies because news is one of the most important things you can post. Who would get the breaking news out first on social media? The B/R higher-ups told us to be first with the news, to basically beat out ESPN and other media outlets. Being first with the news usually gets you the most engagements, even if the source of the news didn't even come from your organization.

B/R would discover breaking news via a tweet by a reporter. Then once the tweet went out, I (for example) would look for an appropriate Getty/AP image and formulate our post on social media. Our news would first get tweeted with "via [news source]" to give credit. The goal was to get out the news on Twitter before ESPN and get the notification out on the Bleacher Report app. Although the writer who broke the news was from ESPN a majority of the time, we had to beat ESPN to posting on our main accounts. Also, we had to get the news right, like the spelling of the player or team's name and tagging the right reporter. I'm not sure if ESPN felt the same tension, but I'm sure they respected the rapidness of our social media and app teams.

Finally, the Social Moments team (B/R's creative team) would compete with ESPN on original content. In content marketing, 'original' means something that hasn't been published online before.[5] There were many times where our Social Moments team would think of unique ideas that would go viral. Creating great original content was one of the main purposes of the team. There was always discussion both positive and negative because we had our eyes on ESPN and what they were doing on social media. A lot of the time, I would see other social media team members chomping at the bit when ESPN rolled out a successful post. Sometimes we could get a little cocky and would compare our posts to theirs, noting how ours did a better job in execution. There were highs and lows but saying there was tension between the two companies is an understatement.

ESPN was and still is Goliath, and Bleacher Report was David. But David had an all-star team of innovators on their Social Moments team. A mix of creative thinkers, former comedians, graphic designers, animators, and video editors. Not saying we won during that 2015–2018 period when I was there, but there were certainly numerous wins along the way. Even though there was tension, there was also respect for ESPN because even though we had a couple stones to throw at Goliath, they were still huge and never quite went down.

"I'll never say that ESPN really had to catch up the most because no matter what they're doing, they're still ESPN. We used to watch them do similar things in real time and realize we were doing similar things, but of a higher quality," former deputy editor of Social Moments at B/R Joey Merkel.[6]

Although Bleacher Report might have had those original content wins, I learned through research and interviews with former ESPN employees that they were true pioneers in sports social media.

GABE GOODWIN'S IMPACT ON SOCIAL MEDIA AT ESPN

In 2009, ESPN launched the show *SportsNation,* which garnered the attention of a younger audience. "Network researchers say it has the youngest, most male audience of any regularly aired program on any ESPN network."[7]

First Take was another up-an-coming show for ESPN. Because of the younger audience of both shows, they were perfect to incorporate a social media element like tweets on air. "In 2009, as *First Take* and *SportsNation* become the shows that use social media best in my opinion at ESPN, and then everything kicked off right around that time," Former ESPN producer Gabe Goodwin of shows *SportsNation* and *First Take.*[8]

Social media was more than just tweeting or posting on Facebook; it could also live on the TV screens. "Social media was not just what you put on social media; it was also how you integrated social media into television," former ESPN employee Michael Bucklin said.[9]

Before the ESPN higher-ups bought in, they expressed uncertainty about where in the company social media belonged. Was it part of the TV production team or part of the marketing team? There was a mix of social media content coming from both teams. The TV production team would promote segments from the shows, and the marketing team would promote broadcasts and public relations activity. Eventually, a balance developed between the two teams, but as you will see, it took a few years to figure it out.

In February and March 2009, *SportsNation* and *First Take* launched their Twitter accounts, respectively. These were pivotal moments in both show's histories because employees who worked for those shows generally ran these accounts instead of a social media team managing those accounts, which would come later.

Before social media was its own team at ESPN, the accounts were run by show producers. I know, way to add more to a producer's plate, but it was just another necessary part of the job. Goodwin had to manage both show's social media accounts, while producing each episode of both shows.

"I never stopped being a TV producer. So I took on social media, as well as being a producer of *SportsNation*. I was making a TV show while also running the Twitter account. I was prepping the talent for a TV show while also teaching them how to better use Twitter. I was always thinking about TV with social media, which caused a lot of friction, frankly, at ESPN," Goodwin said.[8]

Goodwin was a segment producer in 2009 for ESPN shows, but by 2011 his title turned into producer and social media strategist for *SportsNation* and *First Take*. He would produce those two shows, track down tweets for segments on those broadcasts, and also post on social to promote the shows.

"The one thing that absolutely changed everything was the show *SportsNation*. Goodwin had this belief that was very impactful in how we approach social, which was different than a lot of shows were doing it. He believed that the TV show was one hour, and social media was the other 23 hours a day, which meant that social media needed to be original," Bucklin said.[9]

Later on, Goodwin and other producers had success with doing both jobs (producer and social media strategist), which turned into the social production team in 2012.

"It rose up from *SportsNation* and the production team took over *First Take*. *First Take* had just as much if not more success when that show was revamped using social," Goodwin said. "Suddenly I had a team, and we were called 'social production.' That's when we then took over all the shows that were produced out of Bristol,"[8] which is the headquarters of ESPN are located.

There was friction because the higher-ups didn't see the future of social media and what team it belonged in. That friction at ESPN slowly faded away, which opened up the opportunity for a new team for the company. Goodwin was promoted to senior director of social production to lead this new team. Although ESPN didn't have a full-time social media team yet, their social production team would take care of on-camera producing and behind-the-scenes social media.

"We use Facebook to push video in ways no one had before at ESPN. We produce content with talent and the producers of the shows instead of marketing or digital in ways that no one at ESPN had before. A whole team of people is formed from that. Obviously, I'm not alone in that, but I was the leader of that team," Goodwin said.[8]

Other social media employees at ESPN noticed the growth of the social production team and how it transformed the company in their way of thinking.

"I think that's when we were at our best there: when we were housed in production and we had the coverage of our leaders in production. When we were in the social production world, I think we were able really to focus on new content ideas for the social space and that's kind of set up ESPN to where it is today," former director of digital at ESPN Steve Braband said.[10]

ESPN was really innovative because of their use of production mixed with social media coverage. They allowed their social media for TV shows to shine. Accounts grew to six and seven figures' worth of followers over time. A good example of this was the launching of *College GameDay*'s Instagram account, which was run by Tim Dwyer at the time. "We were working with Instagram, and they told us we had the fastest handle in sports to go from zero to one hundred thousand followers, and I think it was in one week. It was because his work was so incredible," Bucklin said.[9]

One of Dwyer's posts went viral on the College GameDay account and still might be one of the top social media posts in ESPN history. "We went inside the locker room of the Army-Navy game during the year that the Navy had hand-painted helmets for each different position group. We took a shot of it, and I think it had tens of millions of views and impressions across social channels. That was one where it was like we were really making something click here," Dwyer said.[11] These milestones showed the higher-ups at ESPN that there was major opportunity for social media in the company.

While Turner Sports higher-ups needed convincing to hire social media staff, ESPN used their employees to run social media on top of other show duties. The higher-ups essentially bought in during the early days of Facebook and Twitter to hire and promote people because of the importance of social media to the company and its shows. ESPN continued to grow the social production team until Goodwin left in mid-2015. In a three-year period, ESPN grew the team to around thirty employees.

"Over the course of a few years, we built a team up to about thirty by the time I left that was covering all the handles and serving alongside and helping most of the main talent in Bristol," Goodwin said.[8]

In talking to numerous former and current employees, it is very apparent that Goodwin had an impact on ESPN. "I think he was single handedly the most impactful person at ESPN for driving social media forward," Bucklin said.[9]

Goodwin, Bucklin, and Braband were leaders of the social production team at ESPN, which eventually turned into the social media team. ESPN would later on hire employees to do social media full-time and not have production on top of their daily duties. Separating the two came in 2014/2015 when employees changed their titles from segment producer to social media manager.

Goodwin was a true gamechanger for not only ESPN but for the industry as a whole. Two years after the launch of the social production team at ESPN were the first hires of Turner Sports' social media team. I learned that they sparked the beginning of the sports social media revolution. Other media outlets took notice of ESPN and began to grow their social media teams according to their budgets. Thankfully, because of the decisions made at ESPN in the early 2010s, Turner Sports opened positions to young professionals like me. My present and future career is the clear result of decisions made in the past at ESPN. ESPN was an innovator in the way it approached and executed sports social media in the early 2010s, which still rings true to this day.

CITATIONS:

1. "A Quote By Carl Sagan," Goodreads, 2021, https://www.goodreads.com/quotes/194992-you-have-to-know-the-past-to-understand-the-present.

2. "ESPN-The Worldwide Leader In Sports 2021. Csun.Edu. Accessed March 12. http://www.csun.edu/~ss674899/Espn.htm.

3. "ESPN, Inc. Fact Sheet," ESPN Press Room US, https://espnpressroom.com/us/espn-inc-fact-sheet/.

4. "NBA Announces 9-Year Extension With ESPN, Turner, Through 2025," Sports Media Watch, 2014, https://www.sportsmediawatch.com/2014/10/nba-tv-deal-espn-abc-tnt-nine-year-deal-2025-24-billion-lockout/.

5. Alicia P, "What Is 'Original Content' And Why Is It Important?" Contentwriters Blog, 2019, https://contentwriters.com/blog/the-importance-of-using-original-content/.

6. Joey Merkel, phone call with author, January 22, 2021.

7. David Barron, "Beadlemania Hits ESPN's Sportsnation," Chron. 2011, https://www.chron.com/entertainment/article/Beadlemania-hits-ESPN-s-SportsNation-1685190.php.

8. Gabe Goodwin, phone call with author, January 11, 2021.

9. Michael Bucklin, phone call with author, January 8, 2021.

10. Steve Braband, phone call with author, January 19, 2021.

11. Tim Dwyer, phone call with author, January 20, 2021.

CHAPTER 4:

SOCIAL MEDIA IS MORE THAN POSTING

"The majority of people that aren't in sports social media think, 'Oh, all they're doing is just like tweeting GIFs or tweeting videos or tweeting memes,' but there's so much behind the scenes that people don't realize," —Social Media Marketing Specialist at DraftKings Josh Handszer said.[1]

When I landed my first job in sports social media at Turner Sports, I'll admit I was a bit naive about all that goes into social media. I wasn't trained in social media at Indiana University. I didn't have a social media internship during the summers between college semesters. I wasn't well versed in social media and all that goes into it. I'm thankful that Turner Sports took a chance on me because I didn't have the experience they might've been seeking.

I was fresh out of a college with a journalism degree and a deep understanding of how to write sports articles. Essentially I was a trained journalist in college with no knowledge of social media. I just thought, "I like social media, and this sounds like a cool position with a major media conglomerate."

I stepped onto the Turner Sports campus in Atlanta with big eyes and an open mind. I wanted to learn as much as possible and be that sponge my parents taught me to be. This was my first corporate job, and I didn't want to mess it up. As I walked into the campus on my first day, the sun was shining, birds were chirping, and big buildings were everywhere. I walked into the building where my team was housed excited to be a part of the first social team at Turner Sports.

I learned everyone's role on the team and didn't realize all the different jobs it took to run a successful social media account.

The nine T3s were brought in because we had a skillset. Plus as Dewan said on the Brand Story Inc. podcast, we were "endemic to the social media space. A T3 is basically a super intern. It's somebody who is given an eleven-month contract, and they have to be two years out of school or less. So we had a base of people that were really helping us starting to program."[2]

In the first month or two of the programs, the other two social media editors and I posted tons and tons of content on Facebook, Twitter, Vine, and YouTube. This was our job: post content from Turner Sports' NBA TV and NBA on TNT to our social media accounts every day and night. Sometimes I would have the 9:00 a.m.–5:00 p.m. shift, and other times I would have the exciting 4:00 p.m,–2:00 a.m. shift. I'm not being sarcastic; it was fun to work late nights sometimes and get paid to watch NBA games. I was really living the dream because I was doing what I always wanted to do: work in sports!

The work I was doing quickly opened my mind to realizing I was do-ing more than just posting. There's a lot of work you need to do to be suc-cessful in this field and grow your account's following. First, you need to consume a lot of video content. By that I mean you have to watch a lot of original programming on the networks and keep an eye on several games per night. Seems easy because it's sports, but depending on what was going on, it wasn't at times.

One night while I was working, we had fourteen games being played. It was my job to watch these various games and look for the best clips for social media. I was the only social media editor working that night, and I had to learn how to multitask to be successful, from watching those games on TV to looking through Twitter and Vine for highlights to watching our live broadcast on NBA TV. Not going to lie: on those nights with all those games to watch, I was probably sweating a bunch because there was a lot on my plate. Took me time to get a process down, but I figured out how to be nimble when stressed with work.

After you consume all that content, you need to grab the best clips for social media. Grabbing the clip means taking it off the broadcast, for which we used SnappyTV, a live TV software where you could essentially grab and edit clips from a broadcast to post directly on social media. It was very innovative to me at the time. This process took time, first editing the clip perfectly then figuring out what worked for our audience and what didn't.

STRATEGY ADAPTS BASED ON THE CONSUMPTION HABITS OF THE AUDIENCE

There are five primary steps to the job of creating social media content, at least there were during my time at Turner. First, strategy, which required answering questions like "Would our audience like this video?" "Will it perform well on our accounts?" and "Why are we posting this content?" Strategy is crucial for every organization to have because if they don't, they won't have success in sports social media where a lot of accounts post similar content. Usually, a LeBron James windmill dunk isn't just posted by NBA TV or NBA on TNT but also NBA, ESPN, SportsCenter, Sports Illustrated, the Lakers, and other NBA/sports-related accounts. So, you have to stand out with what content you post, your timing, and your voice.

Once you have solidified your strategy from the department head, you have to execute the strategy. Strategy isn't developed overnight; it takes time and planning to find out what works and won't work for an account. A company's strategy can change based upon on the consumption habits of an audience. Consumption habits describe how an audience consumes your content, as in do they like this type of content vs. that kind? It's a very in-depth discussion within most organizations because everyone is trying to beat out the competition and adjust their strategy based upon shifting consumption habits of the audience.

"Social media organizations are constantly evolving. The goalposts seem to move and trying to pivot and come up with a new strategy has always been a fun part of social media. I think in those early days at ESPN, we had coverage to test and learn. Then once we tested and learned, we found what worked, and we were able to have the support to hit the ground running and really make a difference in the company," Braband said.

Braband addressed strategy perfectly. Every social media organization needs to evolve over time. You need to constantly test and learn what works and what doesn't. The more you test, the more you learn, and the more you adapt to the consumption habits of the audience. It's easier to test on social media because it's free to post. Not saying that you should post everything and anything, but be deliberate and find out what's been successful and how you can amplify those successes in the future.

THE IMPORTANCE OF CONTENT CREATION

Next, content is king, as you'll see in the next chapter. Content selection is very important in sports social media: why we posted this dunk vs. that dunk, this touchdown pass vs. that one. Not every piece of content will perform well on social, so you gotta keep plugging away cause the next post could overperform. It's all about having the right eye for content and not everyone has this. To have the right eye for content, you need to know what your company wants to post and think of/gather the best content that engages the audience. When considering a piece of content, it needs to be funny, impactful, and connect with the audience. Not every person has the eye for what the audience is looking for or knows how to come up with ideas to engage the audience. Also, understanding the company's strategy then best executing their plan is crucial. What type of content is being posted? Posting the right types of content can do better than other pieces of content.

You not only need to understand why you are posting that piece of content, but also what you are posting in the first place. The "why" is strategy, and the "what" is content. There is a variety of content that I will go in depth about later in this book, but there are three types of content that stand out for me. The three are original content, curated content, and branded content. Each has its own importance in the sports social media world.

"Put simply, original content is content created by you!"[6] Simple enough, right? At Turner Sports, we would create original content each night. During every worknight, there would always be a graphic designer sitting next to me ready to create graphics for our social media accounts. On any given night, a player would "go off" or have an amazing game. Almost every time that happened, I would say to my graphic designer, "We need an original graphic to show his stats from that game." We were creating original content because we were creating content that no other media outlet had. With all the saturation that happens in the newsfeed, original content is what separates you from the competition. Tons of people are endlessly posting the same old content, so you need to be different to engage the audience. Original content helps you stand out because people are looking for something new and fresh in a sea of the same old thing.

"Curated content is content created by others that you select to share with your own audience."[7] This type of content was very important to us at Bleacher Report. We would search Instagram, Twitter, and Facebook for content that would resonate with our audience, checking the accounts of sports fans around the world. Oftentimes, fans would send content directly to our account. If we liked the content, we would ask them how to tag them on social and repost their content. Simple as that.

"Branded content is content that does not involve traditional advertising. It can include articles, videos, podcasts, and even live elements that bring relevant value to the consumer."[8] Branded content will try to include a paid sponsor that backs that piece of content, but the account will try to integrate the brand into the post. Before branded content was popular, an account would post sponsored content, which really was front-facing to the audience, and it could be seen an obnoxious to an audience because it wasn't original or curated content. All three kinds of content have their own way of attracting your current audience and growing your potential audience.

THE DIFFERENCE IN VOICE BETWEEN NBA TV VS. NBA ON TNT

When you're ready to post the content, you have to decide if your voice matches what the organization wants to portray to the public. Some companies I've been at want a conservative voice. Some want a personal voice with emojis, and some want humor. It all depends on what the senior leadership wants, and we execute that strategy on social. "As the industry was evolving beyond 'the social media intern firing off some tweets,' our challenge was to expand our content strategy to drive business goals and develop an organizational voice." former director of digital content at media at the Philadelphia 76ers Charlie Widdoes said.[3] Having an organizational voice sets the tone and helps the audience understand what to expect from your account. In my experience, most accounts don't all of a sudden go from conservative to humorous unless there's a major decision made by one of the higher-ups. By higher-ups, I mean the directors, vice presidents, chief marketing officers, and other high-ranking decision-makers in an organization. In my opinion, the humorous and personal voice best relates with the audience.

Wherever I've worked, I've always asked about the voice we want for the accounts in the first week, so the other social media editors/managers and I could be aware of the tone and cadence of the account. It's important to establish this at an early stage because we are a front-facing part of the organization. It's the way to the organization connects to the audience, makes them fans, and keeps them loyal among the competition in the sports social media world.

A perfect example about the importance of talking about voice occurred during my time at Turner Sports. During my contract, I helped manage four separate accounts: NBA TV, NBA on TNT, March Madness (during the tournament), and PGA.com. Each account had its own voice that the higher-ups wanted to portray to the audience. Two accounts that stood out to me in their contrast of voice was NBA TV vs. NBA on TNT. NBA TV was supposed to be very straightforward with the audience. Our following was mainly diehard NBA fans from around the world. We represented the league, so we weren't too humorous or too serious either, sharing mainly breaking news tweets and highlight packages with players stats in the captions and adding to segments from the channel with an almost buttoned-up voice.

However, the NBA on TNT voice was supposed to have an edge, be funny, and be relatable. It was important to have a voice and tone "similar to Shaq and Charles Barkley" as Dewan would say. Our captions had to be short and to the point but also playful at times. There are segments called "Shaqtin' A Fool" in which Shaq would make fun of random things players did on the court. Our captions needed to mimic the silly mannerisms of

Shaq in these segments. Like "Oh, Boy! Who messed up and made Shaqtin' A Fool this week?" "Come on now! What did JaVale McGee do this time?" We had to add to the video by using humor but also let the video shine on its own too.

Not gonna lie: I more enjoyed working NBA on TNT every Thursday night than working NBA TV every other night.

LISTEN TO THE ANALYTICS

Finally, analytics are an important part of understanding which of your posts were successful. They are more than just numbers; they can give you information on your account's growth of followers, increase of key metrics for the organizations, and break down how your account could be doing better. The numbers are instant feedback from the audience that takes longer in other mediums. The TV industry has the Nielsen ratings, which primarily measure viewing numbers with electronic meters that track what the televisions are tuned to.[4] Analytics can help readjust the strategy to improve the organization's plan to engage their following. "If you don't have analytics, you can't support that one way or the other. You might have five experiments, and four fail, but you have one that works, and then you're able to build off of that one," House of Highlights General Manager Doug Bernstein said.[5]

A man by the name of Luis Alberto Urrea once said "Numbers never lie."[9] In the matter of analytics in social media, they usually don't. They tell a story about an account and how its followers are reacting to content on social media. If content is king, then analytics are queen. I say this because content is the one true separator between accounts from sports to beer companies to fast food chains. But analytics is the best way to see how your content is doing against the competition and against your own goals. If you don't know the numbers, you don't know the essence of your account's growth and engagement in the grand scheme of things.

While growing up, I never realized analytics were a thing. Of course, I saw the likes, the followers, the comments, etc., but I didn't know how it all added up. It's not like I compared my account to my friends' accounts or my engagement with other kids in the classroom. I stayed in my own lane and worried about what I was posting, not what others were doing. It wasn't until I landed at Turner Sports that I recognized that analytics were important to an organization. At that company, we had five out of thirteen people focused on the numbers. We would have weekly meetings using analytics tools to go over our successes and areas needing improvement. This would advertently affect the content we were posting because it justified why some content worked for our audience and some didn't. I learned a ton in those weekly meetings, and they made me a better social media editor at the end of the day.

For those ignorant people and haters of social media managers around the world, just realize that our job isn't easy and not everyone can do it. Not everyone can handle the pressure of a thousand- or million-follower account. Not every person with the power of the keyboard has what it takes to survive and advance in this field and that's okay. It may seem like all fun and games, but it's not. It's a constant battle in your head of "Will this post be successful?" "Will my manager or boss look down upon me for posting this content?" and "I hope my teammates trust my ability to post the right things."

Social media is way more than just posting. There's a lot of things that go into social media that the audience doesn't see. I hope my words can help you see the bigger picture. There are people behind the scenes that are strategizing, planning out the content calendar, figuring out what content works well, working to make sure our voice connects with the audience, and studying what the analytics will say about our account this week. If you're a person who has all the skills necessary to take the bull by the horns, then this job may be for you. Just realize when you land a job in this field, your main goal should be to make a lasting impact on the audience and replicate that success day after day.

CITATIONS:

1. Josh Handszer, phone call with author, December 4, 2020.

2. Sharman, Jay. "Turner Sports—Morgan Dewan." Brand Story Inc., May 5, 2020. Podcast, MP3 audio.

3. Charlie Widdoes, phone call interview with author, January 26, 2021.

4. Seamus Kirst, "What Are Nielsen Ratings And How Are They Calculated?" Forbes, 2021, https://www.forbes.com/sites/seamuskirst/2015/12/18/what-are-nielsen-ratings-and-how-are-they-calculated/?sh=5b314f2d56e0.

5. Doug Bernstein, in-person interview, June 19, 2019.

6. "How To Write Original Content (And Why)," Thrivehive, 2021, https://thrivehive.com/the-importance-of-original-content/.

7. Christina Newberry, "Content Curation: How To Do It The Right Way (Plus Tips And Tools)," Social Media Marketing & Management Dashboard, 2020, https://blog.hootsuite.com/beginners-guide-to-content-curation/.

8. "Branded Content: The What, Why, When, And How," Mission, 2018, https://medium.com/the-mission/branded-content-the-what-why-when-and-how-fb9426dc3e14.

9. "Luis Alberto Urrea Quote: 'Numbers Never Lie, After All: They Simply Tell Different Stories Depending On The Math Of The Tellers,'" Quotefancy, Accessed February 5, 2021, https://quotefancy.com/quote/2291325/Luis-Alberto-Urrea-Numbers-never-lie-after-all-they-simply-tell-different-stories.

CHAPTER 5:
CONTENT IS KING

"Content is King."[1]

I don't remember who first said this to me, but it really resonated with me in regard to my sports social media career over the last eight-plus years. I googled this saying and found out Bill Gates wrote an essay titled "Content is King" in 1996. In 1996, it would've been hard to imagine the sheer scope of content that is available on the web today, but Gates, as usual, was ahead of the curve. This saying still remains true to this day. "Content is King" was a major part of my sports social media education and is still a big pillar of my social media success.

"When it comes to an interactive network such as the internet, the definition of 'content' becomes very wide," Gates said in the "Content is King" essay.[1]

In my time of working in sports social media, content has been the true differentiator between competitors.

Content can have many meanings as I learned when I googled the word. According to Merriam-Webster, content means "something contained, satisfied, to appease the desires of" and numerous other definitions.[2] I couldn't find a definition that relates to social media, but I did find a quote/definition from Olivier Blanchard, a French economist, resonated with me: "The thing about the term 'content' is that it's just vague enough to mean everything and anything, which is to say it doesn't mean anything at all. It's essentially a word that means 'stuff to fill an empty space with.' It could be photos, video, marketing copy, thorough analysis, poetry, farts, vacuous nonsense, cat hair, or cheese cubes."[3]

It's not the perfect definition of what I think content is, but it's not too far off. In the social media world, content could be a video, picture, graphic, gif, animation, cartoon, meme, livestream, etc. There are many types of content in the sports social media world. I learned that quickly during my time working at Bleacher Report (B/R). Our thirty-plus-person social media team would create anything listed above to resonate with and engage the audience. Memes were especially a big deal for B/R because it was what the company was being known for. Not just posting breaking news or sponsored videos, but humorous content played well to our following.

Content is so important in the sports social media world because the newsfeed of every platform is overly saturated with content these days. Sports social media has competitors vying for the consumption of the audience. B/R vs. ESPN vs. Sports Illustrated vs. FOX Sports vs. NBC Sports and on and on.

More accounts get started every day, which will continue to add to the already vast sea of content. Ninety-five million photos and videos are shared on Instagram per day.[4] It doesn't surprise me that there's that much content shared per day, since there over one billion monthly active users on the platform.[5] This is why your content needs to stand out in an ocean filled with random accounts.

If you read the essay "Content is King," you will notice that what he said in 1996 applies to today's world. Bill Gates is simply a genius and maybe a bit of a Nostradamus for our times. There are numerous quotes from that essay that connected with me and my profession as a sports social media specialist.

The first line of the essay rings true in today's world:

"Content is where I expect much of the real money will be made on the internet, just as it was in broadcasting."[1]

Gates was right! The internet is one of many places where money can be made. Whether it's a sponsored social media post, a subscription of Netflix, or an Instagram ad that "somehow" knows you were just browsing the Nike website, all those are forms of paid media and how money is made in the world. Specifically referring to a sponsored social media post is what's called branded content or sponsored content. "'Branded content' falls under 'owned media' because it is shared on channels a brand owns and controls, while 'sponsored content' falls under 'paid media' as a paid media placement."[6] They are different types of content, but both are important to companies or people making money on social media.

I'll never forget what my friend said to me when I launched my social media consulting business: "You need to make money to keep the business afloat." Seems simple enough. If they want to generate revenue in sports social media, companies need followers and for those people to engage with the content. Revenue doesn't just come out of thin air; it's executed because a brand comes to an account in order to post content that engages a new following compared to the brand's existing following.

Nowadays, social media ads are the norm, even though most of the millennials and Gen Zers probably despise this. It's just the way it is. Get used to it! Ads help keep numerous social media managers/editors/coordinators employed because businesses need money to survive.

During my time at B/R, we would often have to post content that was sponsored by Old Spice, Yeti, Coors Light, Nike, McDonalds, Gatorade, and State Farm to name a few. Did I know how much these companies were paying for the ability to be on B/R's account? No. But I did know we were making revenue from each post on each platform. As time went on, every major company I worked for was using social media to post branded or sponsored content because it continued to become more of a revenue driver. We didn't do any sponsored content that I can think of at Turner Sports in 2014, but by 2016 at Bleacher Report, it was a very important revenue stream.

"One of the exciting things about the internet is that anyone with a PC and a modem can publish whatever content they can create."[1]

If only Bill Gates knew in 1996 that almost everyone would have a smartphone in 2021. Social media is just a platform for publishing and distribution to the masses. Literally anyone can publish whatever content they want to the world. This allows the exciting opportunity that all you need is the internet or even data to publish to any social media platform. It allows an exciting opportunity for anyone to contribute to the conversation, to show a part of their lives or interests to their following and the rest of the world.

With public relations, companies or people would pay a public relations professional to get out their news or a story about the company or person out to the media. Social media affords the opportunity for someone to share their story with the world with a click of a button. But even though there's a major positive to posting any types of content on social media, there are negatives too.

"Creating content is a very brave activity. You're putting your work out into the world, and it can be seen by millions of people. If you screw up, they can screengrab it, and they can put it up on a website and slander you over it," VP of Digital Content at FOX Sports Michael Bucklin said.[7] In 2015, the Texas Rangers, an MLB team, misspelled the word "fourth" when referring to "May the Fourth Be With You" on Star Wars Day.[8] This grammatical error was noticed by hundreds if not thousands of people and screenshot numerous times before the team took down the tweet. This mistake should've been caught before the tweet and Facebook post were posted, but it wasn't. Mistakes happen in sports social media, and people online can be ruthless at times. I always say that it's best to have a short-term memory when you're working in sports social media. You always have to be ready for criticism and have a thick skin in this industry.

These ideals of "Content is King" became very evident during my tenure at Bleacher Report. In late 2015 when I got there, I was the fifth team member of our social media team.. Building our social media presence was like sending the first mission to the moon; it was new, there were only five of us, and nobody had any idea of what was to come. Today, the company has over thirty social media team members.

As we hired more people for our B/R social media team in late 2016/ early 2017, the "Content is King" concept became more evident. Our team even learned the phrase "content buckets." It's not a hoop in the Bleacher Report office where if one of our posts/content went viral, we would take a shot at it (even though we did have an awesome half-court basketball hoop in our office). Here's what "content buckets" means to my understanding:

"Content Buckets" are a series of topics that B/R higher-ups signify as important things to post on social media. The "Content Buckets" I used to posting daily were breaking news, graphics, video edits, sponsored posts, high-end animation like "Game of Zones," etc. I'm sure the "Content Buckets" have evolved and continue to evolve as a company like Bleacher Report changes with the times. If "content is king" is the notable saying in the sports social media, "content buckets" are a filtered down version that most sports social media teams think about on a daily basis.

> *"The internet also allows information to be distributed worldwide at basically zero marginal cost to the publisher."*[1]

Any information from a social media user can be distributed for free. Maybe one day these social media platforms will charge for a premium subscription, but for now it's free to create an account on Facebook, Instagram, Twitter, YouTube, TikTok or any other platform. Any information created on that account will be distributed to the world. Certainly, it depends on the hashtags used, accounts tagged, geotagging, or reposting by other accounts to see if that post would get seen by more eyeballs.

"Content is king, but having good content is meaningless unless people are given the means to access it. If ideas aren't taken to market, what good are they? It is the content plus access plus the mediums in which you share them on and owning the rights to the mediums that truly adds value to your content," co-founder of Sports 1 Marketing Dave Meltzer said.[9]

I would always say throughout my career that it's free to post, so have fun with it. If your post doesn't do well, then it's a learning lesson for the social media team and maybe the strategy changes. But at the end of the day, not every post will go viral, and that is okay! Don't always seek out viral for your posts. Seek posts that overperform or do better than your average engagements. "Overperform" is a term we used when I started at Turner Sports and means that the post did better than the average number of interactions a post normally gets for the account.

While at Turner Sports and B/R, we would use this analytics tool called CrowdTangle. It's a tool that allows any person on social media the ability to see how their posts are doing compared to the average interactions of a post. "The result was a dashboard that any publisher could use to see what was working—and what wasn't—on Facebook, Twitter, Instagram, and Vine."[11] A perfect tool to make analytics information more digestible to any social media user because of the simplicity of it. CrowdTangle was started in 2012 and just four years later, it was sold to Facebook.[11]

"Over time, the breadth of information on the internet will be enormous, which will make it compelling."[1]

Social media has turned into a fascinating world of its own. Good or bad, there's a ton of information passed around daily. I'm not sure that number is quantifiable, but I believe it's in the hundreds of millions of posts per day. It is indeed enormous, Mr. Gates! The world of social media ceases to amaze me. That's where the millennials and Gen Zers are constantly hooked to their phones because social media controls their attention and creates an almost addiction to the platforms. "People generally spend an average of three hours and 15 minutes on their phones every day, with the top 20% of smartphone users spending upwards of four and a half hours. On average, we pick up our phones 58 times a day."[12]

The "breadth of information" is what makes social media so exciting at times. You can learn a lot of a lot of things on social media and spend a lot of time using it. Whether your parents like that or not, that's just the way it is. Future generations will grow up with social media accounts and become experts in the ability to use any platform for public consumption. As Bucklin told me, he learned from head of US sports at Twitter TJ Adeshola that there is so much content that you have to be a "timeline stopper."[7]

"You have to stop them with content that is compelling, that makes them want to engage with it in a public fashion and even show their friends.

You've got to be really damn good to get someone to do that. I think a lot of people take that for granted," Bucklin said.[7]

Content creation is a big part of the social media posting process. You need to be thoughtful about what the audience's interests are and cognizant of their attention span. Bucklin believes the audience does still have an attention span that is longer than what most people think. According to an Oberlo article, "Generation Z has an attention span of about 8 seconds. That's a few seconds shorter than the attention span of millennials, which is about 12 seconds. This means that when it comes to marketing to Gen Z, every moment counts."[13] But Bucklin calls BS on Gen Z having a short attention span. "At FOX Sports digital, we just finished 2020 with 19.7 billion minutes of consumption. Attention span is not going anywhere. It's that we have to create content that holds their attention. We believe we're doing that as a strength of ours."[7]

Although I firmly believe "Content is King," there's more to social media than just content. What I've learned throughout my social media career is that there's a lot of thought process behind the posts you see on your news feed. Not only that, but brand analysis, strategy, content creation, branded content, and analytics are just a few parts that make the machine run. These are all principles of sports social media that I currently use to sell as services in my social media consulting business. All these principles will continue to be described, analyzed, and broken down into digestible information.

"People say content is king, but how do we know it's king? The only way for us to know it's king is to see how it performs," Assistant AD of Creative Solutions at Clemson University Athletics Tyson Hutchins said.[14]

Not only is content king, but my next chapter describes how important original content is in today's world. It's vital to have people on your team that can think and create unique content. You are constantly competing with numerous accounts for the audience's attention, so don't be afraid to take risks when it comes to original content. As Dewan told me, "Anybody who thinks sports social media is just a bunch of interns getting on to tweet doesn't have a full sense of how it's run. Social media is a real business."[15]

CITATIONS:

1. Bill Gates, "Bill Gates's Web Site—Columns," Web.Archive, 1996, http://web.archive.org/web/20010126005200/http:/www.microsoft.com/billgates/columns/1996essay/essay960103.asp

2. Merriam-Webster, s.v. "content (n.)," 2021, https://www.merriam-webster.com/dictionary/content.

3. Kim Moutsos, "Content Definition: Sorting It Out," Content Marketing Institute, 2018, https://contentmarketinginstitute.com/2018/03/content-definition/.

4. Mary Lister, "33 Mind-Boggling Instagram Stats & Facts For 2018," Wordstream, 2019, https://www.wordstream.com/blog/ws/2017/04/20/instagram-statistics.

5. Christina Newberry, "44 Instagram Statistics That Matter To Marketers In 2021," *Social Media Marketing & Management Dashboard,* 2021, https://blog.hootsuite.com/instagram-statistics/.

6. Shaye Dipasquale, "The Difference Between Branded, Sponsored, Native, And Content Marketing - Ed2010," *Ed2010,* 2021, https://ed2010.com/generic/unsolicited-advice/the-difference-between-branded-sponsored-native-and-content-marketing/.

7. Michael Bucklin, phone call with the author, January 8, 2021.

8. Josh Criswell (@Item_Criswell), "Texas Rangers completely botch Star Wars Day (Photos)," Twitter, May 4, 2015.

9. Dave Meltzer, phone call with the author, October 27, 2020.

11. Casey Newton, "Facebook Buys Crowdtangle, The Tool Publishers Use To Win The Internet," The Verge, 2016, https://www.theverge.com/2016/11/11/13594338/facebook-acquires-crowdtangle.

12. Adrienne Matei, "Shock! Horror! Do You Know How Much Time You Spend On Your Phone?" The Guardian, Accessed March 13, 2021, https://www.theguardian.com/lifeandstyle/2019/aug/21/cellphone-screen-time-average-habits.

13. Thomas Law, "10 Vital Strategies To Use When Marketing To Generation Z In 2020," Oberlo, 2020, https://www.oberlo.com/blog/marketing-strategies-generation-z.

14. Tyson Hutchins, phone call with the author, January 28, 2021.

15. Morgan Dewan, phone call with the author, November 3, 2020.

CHAPTER 6:

ORIGINAL CONTENT IS THE TRUE DIFFERENTIATOR

"You have to have original content in order to be successful because your audience's eyeballs are all going online. If you want to stay young and you want to stay relevant, you have to have original content to keep that brand of business alive," —former social media director of the UFC Randy Faehnrich[1]

Bill Gates's 1996 essay is still ringing in my ears, and hopefully in yours too, because it's what makes you a player in the game of sports social media. It is what makes a sports social media team stand out in today's world. The type of content that will differentiate you from your competition is original content. Content is what drives companies and people to interact with an audience, to amass followers and, therefore, profit. But with nearly every company out there doing it, how do you stand out among the crowd? The answer is deceptively simple: be original. "In content marketing, 'original' means something that hasn't been published online before."[2] Wherever I've worked in my career, original content was the utmost important content we relied on.

Turner Sports relied on original programming, specifically from NBA on TNT's *Inside the NBA* show. When I worked Thursday nights, the original content was golden. Quotes galore from Shaq, funny moments between Shaq and Charles Barkley, and great basketball insight from Kenny "The Jet" Smith. Segments like "Shaqtin' A Fool," "EJ's Neat-O Stat of the Night," and "Who He Play For?" were the perfect moments for our social media accounts. Posting these clips would lead to overperforming posts and would go viral every now and then. The humor was unmatched in original sports television programming. Since about 2006, it's been my favorite sports show on TV. In case you were wondering, the show has been running since 1989 and has won eleven Sports Emmy Awards. It's easy to see why it's so highly regarded in sports television history.

When I went to Bleacher Report, creating original social media was our bread and butter. It's one of the things that made B/R what it is today. B/R's original content team was called the Social Moments team, created in late 2015 and dedicated to making original content that connected with and engaged the audience. Although I was on the Social Programming team and not the Social Moments team, I tried to contribute ideas if I could. I revered that team. I would send ideas to people on the team as if I were a little schoolboy sending notes to his crush in the middle of class. What can I say? They were constantly cooking up viral moments, and I wished I were a part of that team. I wanted my shot to create original content idea that went viral. I know I wanted a bit of an ego boost, but so what? I was creative and wanted to contribute outside-the-box ideas. B/R was growing a rapid following for funny, interesting, engaging, original social media moments. As you'll see in a later chapter on B/R, this was the team that really distinguished the company in the social media world.

Not long after returning to Los Angeles, I landed a position with the NFL. Thanks to my former B/R coworker, CJ Toledano, for putting in a good word for me. The purpose of my contract was to manage NFL Network's social media accounts. A coworker of mine and I would create videos to promote the shows on our channel and graphics that would engage the audience. Original content was the only way for our account to stand out in the myriad of NFL-focused social media accounts. One of our main goals of the account was to grow our Instagram page with original content, and we did just that. During my nine-month contract, the IG account grew nearly six hundred thousand new followers (a 35% growth)! We helped the page hit the two-million-follower milestone, which was super gratifying. I wasn't running the main NFL accounts but still had a fun time thinking of ways to differentiate NFL Network from the competition with original content ideas.

Original content is and always will be my favorite type of content. It's those outside-the-box ideas that get my juices flowing. It's more important to me than just reposting a follower account. It's the execution of an idea from its inception to getting posted to seeing how its performing on social. Not every original content idea will go viral, but you keep pushing ahead because it's your job to keep thinking of ideas that will perform well. To not just sit around and wait for sports social media moments to come to you but think of ideas that make your teammates and the company proud. Don't forget that social media is a front-facing part of the business. Our tweets and posts are getting seen by thousands if not millions of people. If a sports social media team doesn't have original content, it's not going to keep up with its competition. Original content is one of the key components that makes one company excel over another.

WHAT IS THUMB-STOPPING CONTENT?

In over ninety interviews I did for this for this book, I heard the words "thumb-stopping content" numerous times. I didn't know what it meant because I'd never heard this term before. What I soon learned was that it's more important today than ever. Thumb-stopping content means exactly what it says it is: original content that catches the audience's eye while they are scrolling through the news feed. The content literally wants to make the user stop the scroll and look at what your account posted. Thumb-stopping content is more important than ever because there's a "saturation" of Instagram content, which is what House of Highlights founder Omar Raja told me.[3]

There wasn't such saturation in the past because there were fewer IG accounts. Years into Instagram's growth in the market between 2013–2016, the algorithm was chronological and not based on engagements and how popular your account was. The change happened in mid-2016. Users could no longer get posts in reverse-chronological order, and instead the social network started pushing content to the top depending on the type of content you like and the users you follow."[4] The change really affected those accounts trying to go viral because they would pop up less on someone's news feed than it would in the past.

It's interesting because in a 2020 PC Mag article, "Instagram is testing a reverse-chronological 'Latest Posts' feature."[4] This would be interesting because it would give accounts with fewer followers the opportunity to show up more on the timeline of any user that follows them. The algorithm of each platform dictates how a sports social media manager will post. You have to take advantage of what the algorithm gives you. A sports social media team is constantly aware of the changes of each platform's algorithm because it impacts your strategy. From my experience, most big sports social media accounts have a direct rep to the platform to get algorithm changes before they go to the general public. Once the team is aware of these changes, so does your strategy change. You've got to roll with the punches.

To take advantage of the algorithm these days, you need to have thumb-stopping content. According to former social media editor at the XFL Zain Pyarali, it was a phrase used often by the entire league. "You want that thumb-stopping content. Everyone out on social media is saying something, posting something. But what are we going to do? What are we going to make is whenever you're scrolling on your phone, on Twitter, or an Instagram or Facebook, that's going to make you stop and look at the content," he said.[5] With the saturation of content, you need to make a piece of original content that really pops, that catches the audience's eyes and gets them to engage with it over your competition's posts. That is the way you stand out in today's social media frenzy world.

Original content is king. What you create, the voice behind it, and the execution of that content is what is most important now and most likely for years to come. While I was at Turner Sports, we had amazing original content all over the place. Broadcasts were filmed in the Atlanta studios where the social media editors would watch and consume the original program and look for bites for our accounts. "It didn't require me going out and spending huge media dollars to have that thumb-stopping power. It was innate in the content; it was just a way of reframing it," Dewan said.[6] All we had to do was capture the original content from TV and post it. Seems easy enough, but you have to have a good eye of what works and what doesn't work on social media to be successful in any role in the industry.

Making original content was also part of my role at Turner Sports. Our team needed to make visually stunning graphics and cool video highlight edits to stand out among the competition. We had a graphic designer always sitting next to us, so that they could make a graphic when needed. Usually, the graphics were to highlight a player who had a big game or stats from a game on our network to shine a spotlight on the score. The social media editors also had to edit video highlights to catch our audience's attention. I had absolutely no video editing experience at the time, but I quickly learned from repetition and being a sponge to the video editors around me.

The type of original content varies depending on what the social media team chooses to make. It's more than just posting a photo these days; you really have to think about what will work for the audience. We don't think of ourselves first in this industry, we think of how the audience will react. "Whether we're making a graphic that's super eye-catching, or we make a video that's super compelling, what can we do to make our users stop and consume our content?" Pyarali said.[5] Because there is so much saturation in the market, your original content must stand out or you can lose to your competitors and fall out of somewhat digital relevance. Social media is front-facing, and the organization will sometimes put the weight on the social media teams' shoulders to produce quality numbers and viral moments.

BLEACHER REPORT MADE COMPETITION RAISE THEIR GAME

Original content was not as relevant to B/R in the first ten years of the company. By 2015, the company was slowly making their way toward being the gold standard for original content in the sports social media world. They were doing this because they hired people in-house to cause a disruption in the industry. They weren't afraid to take risks with memes, head swaps, jersey swaps, video effects, and other forms of original content. Not fearing taking risks is what truly made B/R game changers in the field from 2015–2018. In my opinion, they had more viral moments than any other sports social media account during that time. They were just that good, and other companies noticed it.

One of the main ideators of B/R's Social Moments team was CJ Toledano. Social moments was the team that thought of viral ideas and posts that would catch the audience's eye and make them share it with their friends. "I think that was one of the most groundbreaking teams in terms of creating original content," Toledano said.[8] The makeup of the team truly made it one of the top teams in sports social media as Toledano explained. "We were the team that had a bunch of people who had experience working on accounts, but we were also young and maybe a little bit crazy."[8]

This team was all about creating memes. Memes helped you stand apart from the rest of the competition in sports social media. "A meme is a virally transmitted image embellished with text, usually sharing pointed commentary on cultural symbols, social ideas, or current events."[9] Toledano explained that B/R really cared about creating viral memes. "Bleacher Report was really putting all of their eggs in creating memes. They were one of the first companies that really treated memes seriously. They would say, 'This is like the future of content here.' We were just addicted to having the best piece of content numbers-wise and quality-wise after a big sports moment," Toledano said.[8]

Other companies started noticing B/R's rise to the top of the sports social media food chain. After creating one viral meme after another, I'm guessing it left other media companies in awe of what B/R was doing. "Original content is going to flow from everyone. I think that a company like B/R was at the forefront of it, where they are being very personal and open with the voice," social media marketing specialist at ESPN J'Ron Erby said.[10]

Other companies shared a similar sentiment. "Everyone was like, 'We need to do it like Bleacher.' When I was at STN, we would specifically look at Bleacher and be like, 'How do we create this for the San Francisco Giants or for the Green Bay Packers?'" former senior director of accounts at STN Digital Kris Koivisto said.[11] STN Digital is a social-first marketing agency that works with some of the top brands in the country, including sports teams. Original content was important to Bleacher Report, and the competition noticed and had to step up their game.

Just as ESPN were the leaders of sports social media in the early 2010s, Bleacher Report were the innovators of original content in the mid-2010s. The shift happened because of the mix of hiring talented ideators/creators and the blessing from the higher-ups to innovate in the space. B/R was pushing out one thumb-stopping moment after the next. The Social Moments team was given free rein to create viral memes and memorable moments in sports social media history. There's no doubt that original content is king to B/R.

Original content should be important for all sports social media teams because it will allow you to differentiate yourself from the competition. With the saturation of content comes the need to create original content that will be thumb-stopping; in other words, stop the scroll. In my mind, the recipe for success is the people you hire. They have to be outside-the-box thinkers, competitive content creators, and as Toledano said, "a little bit crazy."[8] Not every person can think of viral original content ideas, and that's okay because everyone brings something to the table.

CITATIONS:

1. Randy Faehnrich, phone call with author, December 28, 2020.

2. Alicia P, "What Is 'Original Content' And Why Is It Important?" *Contentwriters Blog,* 2019, https://contentwriters.com/blog/the-importance-of-using-original-content/.

3. Omar Raja, phone call with author, February 3, 2021.

4. Justin Herrick, "Instagram Tests Reverse-Chronological 'Latest Posts' Feature," *PCMAG,* 2020, https://www.pcmag.com/news/instagram-tests-reverse-chronological-latest-posts-feature.

5. Zain Pyarali, phone call with author, November 18, 2020.

6. Morgan Dewan, phone call with author, November 3, 2020.

8. CJ Toledano, phone call with author, December 23, 2020.

9. Paul Gil, "Examples Of Memes And How To Use Them," *Lifewire*, 2020, https://www.lifewire.com/what-is-a-meme-2483702.

10. J'Ron Erby, phone call with author, December 1, 2020.

11. Kris Koivisto, phone call with author, December 1, 2020.

CHAPTER 7:

USER-GENERATED CONTENT IS A MARKETING GOLDMINE

"User-generated content (UGC) is a marketing goldmine. If you know how to use it, it can create a snowball effect of higher engagement and more social followers," —Neil Patel[1]

To define what UGC is, we need to understand why it's different than original content. Original content is content created by a brand or company that hasn't been posted before. User-generated content (UGC) is any content—text, videos, images, reviews, etc.—created by people rather than brands. And brands will often share UGC on their own social media accounts, website, and other marketing channels."[2] It's important to understand the difference between the user creating content that hasn't been seen before and a brand creating original content. People create user-generated content, so the public has the opportunity to create something that can be seen by the masses because it's public once it's posted.

I believe UGC is right behind original content (but before branded/sponsored content) in the order of importance for sports social media these days. Why? Because UGC allows fans and followers to make content that can get reposted by a major brand. This brings a culture into the sports social media world of people wanting to go viral or submit their video via direct message (DM) to a million-follower account to gain popularity. When the founder of House of Highlights (HoH) Omar Raja was asked about why people create UGC to be reposted by a popular sports social media account, his answer was simple. "I think the big thing is everyone wants to kind of be famous," he said.[3] He couldn't have said it any better.

For one of the younger generations, millennial and Gen Z, going viral is an attainable goal. These generations want to grow their following and get recognition from their friends. "They want to send their play to House of Highlights or wherever, and they want it posted, and they want all their friends be able to see it. They want to be able to brag about it," Omar said.[3] Bragging rights is big among friends. I know my friends used to talk about how many points they scored in a basketball tournament in sports camp growing up. Now, kids and teenagers are bragging over their video being reposted by a major account. It's a competition, and just like with sports, not everyone wins. There will still be that same high when being reposted by a major account because it's instant recognition that you posted something noteworthy, and your friends will give you the praise as well.

The easy way to grow your hundred or so follower account is to get reposted by a credited account with multi-million followers. You get re-posted and tagged in the caption by the account, which drives the masses to your profile resulting in hundreds if not thousands of new followers. This happened to me when I captured a video of Floyd Mayweather throwing money at Conor McGregor during their 2017 prefight press conference at the Barclays Center in Brooklyn. I recorded the video (while I was working for Bleacher Report), then I was reposted by HoH, and my handle was tagged in the caption. As soon as that happened, thousands of people requested to follow me on Instagram (because I was private at the time), and I received nonstop attention from the masses over the next twenty-four-plus hours. I had friends from high school and even a teacher from middle school reach out to me. I felt that high from all the attention I was receiving, but it was short-lived as the time cycle for the Instagram feed was usually 24 hours at the time.

Getting reposted by a sports social media account with a major following isn't easy. When I was at B/R, part of my job as a social media programmer was to look through the thousands of DMs we were getting daily to find the one that would make the most sense for our following. Not only DMs, but B/R would also get tagged by thousands of accounts daily to try and get reposted. I wound spend one to two hours of my day looking for videos that would go viral for our account.

Before UGC was a big deal, I would only worry about original content coming from B/R. With UGC, I spent at least six hours a week looking for the next great viral video. The whole team would search, and it became almost a competition between people in the Social Programming team of who could find the top UGC video and how it would perform. We had a running spreadsheet of videos that programmers would find in the DMs or posts we were tagged in. We would assign our name next to the UGC video we found to get credit for the "detective" work. None of us were Sherlock Holmes, but searching for the best UGC was an artform. It was who had the best eye for a potential viral video. You've got to know what your audience is looking for, what will do well with the sports social media audience, and what won't perform well. Not everyone has that eye for finding the next viral UGC video, and I'll admit I was pretty average at it. Although it was time-consuming, I enjoyed the process.

Finding a viral video is a science of perception and anticipation. How well do you know your audience? What are current trends that you can act on? Are you aware of the current sports scene and which memes are going around? You have to take these things into account when looking for the next viral UGC video because if you don't, you could end up with a big social media bust. Some people think going viral is random because of various trendsetters who post something unheard of and generate millions of views, but even those posts are based on the current climate, or they use novelty to generate interest.

A side part of the role was sending over UGC to HoH. If we found a video that their team didn't find, we would send over. But this also turned into a competition as well: if Omar would find a UGC video instead of us that would do well for his HoH account, some of us on the team were envious. He was a one-person team for the first few years of his account, and we had at least five people looking for UGC, sometimes finding the same content as he did. Or there were times where Omar would say, "I saw that video but didn't like it." Omar had an eye for viral UGC and, in my opinion, is the best in the sports social media business at finding those hidden gems. Omar would also pass us UGC content that he thought would fit the B/R account and our following. Although we could be competitive about UGC, we always respected the talent of each account.

THE RISE OF HOUSE OF HIGHLIGHTS THANKS TO UGC

Although Omar wasn't the first person to repost UGC on his account, he did see the value in it. He recognized one of the first platforms to repost UGC: America's Funniest Home Videos (AFHV). The show has a simple premise. People submit funny videos to producers at ABC, and they would air the funniest clips. "In 1989, producer Vin Di Bona sold ABC on the concept that became America's Funniest Home Videos in less than five minutes. And within weeks of its debut as a regular series on ABC in January 1990, Vin Di Bona Productions was receiving about 1,600 videotapes a day."[4] The show soon become a hit and a regular weekly show on ABC. The show has had thirty-one seasons and over seven hundred episodes since launching.

I mention AFHV because they were one of the first groups to take a piece of UGC and repost it by putting it on air. Omar equates being on air on AFHV to being reposted by a major sports social media account. "It's kind of even better than the old days of just being on TV, where your clips make it on America's Funniest Home Videos," he said.[3] There is a sense of pride when it comes to getting your UGC posted on HoH, B/R, ESPN, SportsCenter, or any other major sports social media account. It's a badge of honor, and it might only happen once in a lifetime. So relish in it.

Omar said it's better than AFHV because you can see the instant impact from the numbers on social media. Some videos on B/R and HoH were not getting in the thousands but the millions of views. "You can see how many millions of views it's getting and how many likes it's getting. You can see how people are reacting to it. But you can also see who is reacting to it. A lot of the times it's your favorite player," he said.[3] There's no other platform like Instagram where posts get reposted on it, and your favorite players can engage with it because they follow B/R and HoH. The younger generation of athletes are all following these accounts. No wonder why it would be exciting for a twelve-year-old to be reposted by one of the accounts because of their homemade trick-shot video.

HoH became so well known for reposting UGC that sponsors hopped on board to sponsor videos on the account. Omar told me the first sponsor was Lexus in 2016, where they produced seven to ten videos highlighting UGC. "I'll never forget that one. Where we just got UGC videos and posted it," he said.[3] Seems simple enough, but finding the right the campaign was a success, and that started the ball rolling for HoH to generate revenue from UGC.

Under Armour came knocking and wanted to do a campaign with their top NBA player, Warriors superstar Steph Curry. The campaign was called "The Curry Challenge," where HoH posted clips of ordinary people trying to imitate Curry's moves.[5] They made a video compilation of fans around the world doing their best Curry imitation. The video was a success: 2.8 million views and over 360,000 likes on IG alone. The clip was also narrated by Bob Menery, a well-known sports comedian who got famous for doing faux sports broadcasting on IG. When asked what some examples of brands are working with HoH, Omar responded by saying, "I think my favorite one is probably the Curry Challenge. I think [that's] the best one. I might be wrong here, but it got like 3M views, which in 2017 according to Brandtale, was [one of] the highest viewed branded video on all of Instagram."[6] Amazing how Omar and the HoH team put together a unique branded content video that engaged so highly with their fans.

I don't think branded content videos generally do that well because the audience knows when a brand is sponsoring the content. That usually turns them off because branded content is essentially an ad on social media. As a sports social media account, you have to mask this ad to be more appealing to the audience. But as we all know, every account wants to generate revenue from social media, and not everyone has the right recipe to do so. It takes a both creative and a sales-minded team to best execute on social media. Branded content needs to show a brand without being too overt with the post, and that is an art in itself.

One of the challenges I vividly remember was the "Drive-by Dunk Challenge." Similar to "The Curry Challenge," fans would submit videos via DM and tag HoH to get reposted by the account. In 2017, HoH reposted a video of two teenagers dunking on random people's hoops in their driveway. The first video that launched the challenge received over 1.2 million views and nearly 200,000 likes. Amazing to see a video like this take off, but it did, and the challenge was started. Well-known sports blog Deadspin called it "the meme of the summer." I remember finding videos on Instagram for Omar and HoH team to use. A few were used, but more were denied. As the major sports social media account that started the trend, they needed to be very selective with what they posted. Not every Joe Schmo could get the love from one of the most beloved sports social media accounts in history.

NBA superstar James "The Beard" Harden even participated in the challenge. Harden jumped off a boat in Miami, dunked on a court filled with regular basketball players there, and ran back to the boat to speed off. The video garnered nearly 1.7 million views and 260,000 likes on WorldStar Hip Hop's IG account. "WorldStar Hip Hop is home to everything entertainment & hip hop."[7] Impressive to say the least, and it was all started by HoH. Numerous videos were submitted, and only a handful were selected. Trends happen, and eventually they die down, which is what happened to the "Drive-by Dunk Challenge." But it lasted almost the whole summer.

Not all challenges went viral for HoH, but most did. I just mentioned two that stood out for me even years later. HoH thrived off of UGC. It became important for B/R's account too. I believe that's one of the reasons HoH became so popular. Any person at any time had the chance of getting their video seen by millions of people because of the simple repost by Omar and the HoH team. HoH changed the sports social media industry by making UGC so popular that other major accounts had to follow in Omar's footsteps and post similar content from fans.

THE CONTROVERSY OF ORIGINAL CONTENT VS. UGC

Although UGC was highly regarded at B/R and HoH, original content was seen as a bit higher on the totem pole than UGC in terms of its relevance to the audience. Original content, UGC, and branded content were all parts of B/R's content buckets while I was there, but original content connected with our audience differently than the other two.

Most companies post UGC because their following finds a connection to it. If this person can get reposted on this account with a major following, why can't my content do the same? "Consumers are 2.4x more likely to say user-generated content (UGC) is authentic compared to brand-created content."[8] It is important for every brand to build trust and loyalty with their following, so they can grow them over time while keeping them engaged. UGC is a great way to show authenticity to your audience, which inadvertently helps build loyalty over time.

Everyone has UGC as part of their content bucket because it adds another stream of content for any sports social media account. Every sports social media account needs multiple streams of content to fill the content calendar. The content calendar is a schedule of content that helps spread out the content for each week. Through numerous interviews with sports social media experts, I learned that your account could have UGC for authenticity, but what's most important is really differentiating yourself from the competition with original content.

As Omar said, your account needs to evolve over time. "I think everyone that starts off as a curator has to get to a point where you can make original content and have original ideas," he said.[3] The evolution needs to happen so that your account can progress, and you can reach new audiences to grow your following. "Netflix is the best example of that. Who would have thought in the beginning that Netflix would be the one that has these shows that win Emmys?" he said.[3] Netflix at first brought in content from media conglomerates and then started to create their own original content. HoH started with NBA highlights and UGC but evolved into a Twitter show, YouTube channel, and TikTok account and posted more new forms of original content.

Not everyone believes that UGC, curating, or aggregating content matters as much as original content for an organization. There was pushback in the interviews I conducted about the difference between original content and UGC. Director of social media at Golf Magazine Tim Reilly shared that sentiment. "In a social space, there's always a fine line between aggregators and original content creators. There's a lot of aggregators out there in social media," he said. "Anyone can rip a video and post it. But the people that really stick and resonate with their audience are the ones that are able to make original content. Those are the ones that have the most engaging audience."[9] He makes a good point. Original content separates you from all the aggregators, the people who search for UGC and just repost it without creating any original content themselves. There's a distinct line between these kinds of people or organizations and what they deem important for their account.

On top of that, there will be a curation of the same content over and over by sports social media organizations. Followers will start to see that they see the same video across various sports social media accounts that they follow. It's not unique at that point. It's just an overly saturated news feed. "Everybody is really aggregating the same content, whether it's a happy birthday LeBron or James Harden gained some weight over the quarantine. You have to constantly find your own angle. If not, you can do pretty well, but you're just kind of resharing the same stuff that everybody else does," CEO and owner of STN Digital David Brickley said.[10] So you have to separate yourself from the competition with unique original content that connects with your followers. Brickley mentioned how B/R stood out because of original content like Game of Zones or well-known football player Marshawn Lynch's show. "You really start to become someone that people look up to and also, you start to separate yourself from the pack," he said.[10]

Although UGC is a marketing goldmine because of its authenticity with the audience, it can be frowned upon at times because of the saturation of the news feed in today's world. If you don't stand out in the sports social media space, then you can fall behind. Higher-ups in sports media organizations don't want to fall behind to the competition because it could be hard to recover since the audience will gravitate toward other accounts.

Although most people can have that eye for UGC, not everyone has that eye for original content and what will go viral. Succeeding in an overly saturated sports social media industry all depends on the staff you hire, how creative and hardworking they are. I'm not saying UGC is bad for the industry, but find content that no one is finding and post it first. If you don't, then others will gain more loyalty from their following because they were ahead of the curve. If you're not ten steps ahead of the competition, then you can fall behind and become a less relevant sports social media account to follow. Obviously, no one wants that to happen.

CITATIONS:

1. Neil Patel, "How To Grow Your Social Fans By 400% With User-Generated Content," Neil Patel Accessed February 10, 2021, https://neil-patel.com/blog/user-generated-content/.

2. Christina Newberry, "A Simple Guide To Using User-Generated Content On Social Media" Social Media Marketing & Management Dashboard, 2019, https://blog.hootsuite.com/user-generated-content-ugc/.

3. Omar Raja, phone interview with author, February 3, 2021.

4. Cynthia Littleton, "Putting The Fun In 'Home Videos.' (Vincent John Di Bona, Executive Producer Of Television Program America's Funniest Home Videos) (Fifth Estater) (Column)," *Web.Archive.Org,* 1996, https://web.archive.org/web/20121105171457/http://www.highbeam.com/doc/1G1-18306720.html.

5. Cale Weissman, "Bleacher Report's Secret Weapon Is A 23-Year-Old Instagram Savant," *Fast Company,* 2018, https://www.fastcompany.com/40519104/bleacher-reports-secret-weapon-is-a-23-year-old-instagram-savant.

6. "Q&A: House of Highlights' Omar Raja Talks Getting Clips From All-Stars," *Innovate By Hashtag Sports,* 2018, https://innovate.hashtag-sports.com/2018/08/23/house-of-highlights-omar-raja-nba-stars/.

7. "Worldstarhiphop: Breaking News | Music Videos | Entertainment News | Hip Hop News," Worldstarhiphop.com, Accessed February 11, 2021, https://worldstarhiphop.com/videos/.

8. Business Wire, "Stackla Survey Reveals Disconnect Between The Content Consumers Want & What Marketers Deliver," *Businesswire.com*, Accessed February 11, 2021, https://www.businesswire.com/news/home/20190220005302/en/Stackla-Survey-Reveals-Disconnect-Content-Consumers-Marketers.

9. Tim Reilly, phone call with author, November 23, 2020.

10. David Brickley, phone call with author, December 18, 2020.

CHAPTER 8:

BRANDED CONTENT IS KEY TO GENERATING REVENUE ON SOCIAL MEDIA

"You have to go about this, not about how we
can make a bunch of money, but you do go about
producing great content and the money will come,"
—President and CEO of the Portland Trail Blazers
Chris McGowan[1]

Before social media was a revenue generator, companies were just figuring out how to use the various platforms. There weren't many paid social media opportunities (if any at all) because sponsors wanted to spend their money on TV and digital advertisements. In the early 2010s, they didn't understand the value of social media because it was tough to quantify what they were getting from putting money behind it. On TV, you know you're going to get X number of viewers based on the channel and show. On the internet, you can figure out how much traffic is going to certain websites. With social media, some videos can get views in the thousands, and some can get in the millions. It just depends on your account and how engaged the audience is with it.

In the beginning, advertisers didn't know how much money a social media deal was worth, which sports social media accounts they should put money behind, and what that investment would do for their brand overall.

Over time, the blurred lines have become clearer, but everyone is still trying to figure out where the money is coming from and the impact it has on your following. Sponsored and branded content in sports social media has only been around for about a decade. In order to understand branded content, we first need to break down what sponsored content is. Sponsored content is a piece of content that shows the brand overtly, while branded content integrates the brand into the content.

During my time at Turner Sports in 2014, we didn't post much sponsored content. I'm not sure if we posted any sponsored content on the NBA TV or NBA on TNT accounts that year. The sales team at Turner Sports was focused on selling ad space on our television channels and not on social media. Very few companies had a focus on money from social media. Official sponsored content was nonexistent in the sports social media space.

I noticed a change in my career during the 2015 March Madness tournament. March Madness is the college basketball tournament where sixty-eight teams fight for the crown to be titled champion and get to cut down the nets (a well-respected tradition in sports). Our social media team was tasked with posting all of the sponsored content for the main March Madness account. "Sponsored content is premium content that a sponsor pays a publisher to create and distribute."[2] Each day I would go for my shift in a large auditorium in the Turner Sports campus. It was pretty dark as the room had no windows and just a bunch of TVs that were only on for viewing the games. We worked alongside social media team members from the National Collegiate Athletic Association (NCAA) to put together the best plan for the tournament.

The Turner Sports social media team's purpose was to watch all the games during the tournament, look for moments that would resonate with the audience, and put a paid sponsor behind any clip we saw fit. The NCAA team would handle all the highlights for the account. The sponsors we worked with included Pizza Hut, Axe, and Dove. Each sponsor wanted to look for a certain moment that would make sense for the clip. I believe Pizza Hut wanted a big play moment, Axe wanted a game-winning or clutch shot, and Dove wanted an emotional moment during the game. The social media editors on our team (including myself) would closely watch these games looking for those plays/moments.

Once we found a play that made sense for one of the sponsors, we would edit the clip for social media using SnappyTV (our live TV editing software) and put a paid pre-roll (a sponsor's short call out to themselves) on the video before posting. The tricky part was coming up with the caption. Because it was a paid sponsor for the social media video, we couldn't refer at all to the player in the video. We couldn't say his name, jersey number, school year (freshman, sophomore, etc.), or anything else that would identify any college player in the video. Not only that, but all of our captions had to go through the Turner Sports legal team before posting. They were basically the gatekeepers before our posts went public to the audience. The NCAA didn't want viewers to have any way of connecting the sponsor to the college athlete, even though the NCAA was basically profiting off the players in the tournament. Certainly, the new Name, Image, Likeness (NIL) rules changed, which allowed college athletes to start making money in summer 2021. This is revolutionary for college sports because it allows any athlete to make revenue every time their name, image, or likeness is being used.

That is my best example of our company making revenue from social media during my contract at Turner Sports. I didn't see many cases other than that because the sales team was hyper-focused on generating revenue from the TV channels, ads on websites, and various ad placements on Turner Sports apps. Social media wasn't a viable revenue source in the early 2010s, but things quickly changed in the mid-2010s.

BECKLEY MASON'S IMPACT ON BLEACHER REPORT'S BRANDED CONTENT TEAM

After my time at Turner Sports, I started my social media editor position with Bleacher Report. During my first four to six months, I would say we mixed in some sponsored content with our regular social media posts that pointed to B/R's website. My role in late 2015 was to grab an article from the website and post about it on social media. These posts would drive traffic to the website where there would be sponsored ads placed throughout articles.

This was sponsored content, advertisement that a sponsor would pay to be featured on the B/R website. I would say in early 2016, a noticeable change was the sales team making sure we were tagging a sponsor in a post. Usually, it would be Coors Light who did this series called "Cold Hard Facts." We would post a stat graphic or video that had Coors Light's logo on it, and we had to tag Coors Light and use #ColdHardFacts in the caption. That is a prime example of sponsored content. Seems simple enough, and it was, as long as you didn't mess up the directions from the sales team.

A change at B/R happened in April 2016 when the company hired Beckley Mason, a former writer/editor and producer in the media and agency world. Mason was B/R's first hire focused on branded content. "Branded content is any content where the brand is integrated has an active integration in the execution of the work," Mason said.[3] Mason told me the main difference between branded content and sponsored content is the activity of the sponsor. If a sponsor just wants to slap a logo on a graphic or video or use pre-roll, that falls into sponsored content. Mason told me when the sponsor wants to actively get involved in the execution part of the content, then it turns into branded content. "Once the brand is in a back and forth influencing the execution of the content and you're really making it on their behalf, then that's branded content," Mason said.[3] It's good to distinguish the two because for the longest time, I thought branded content was a subset of sponsored content, but they are different in the sales world.

Mason discussed why his career shifted into branded content was because "it's an interesting problem that's both creative and business minded."[3] First off, as a business, you need to offer different content than your competitors. Next, you have to make creative content that resonates with the audience. "In social media, the real estate that you have is the content itself, Mason said."[3] Mason had to create a sales process that included an infrastructure around pricing, go-to market strategy and more from scratch. "It took us eighteen months from my hire for us to even really start making a serious dent. And then from that moment to today, which is about three years later, we have become a third of Bleacher Report's direct revenue," Mason said.[3] Mason had to hire numerous people for the branded content team to be successful.

Mason discussed his favorite branded content projects during his five-year career with B/R. He brought up a campaign the company did with Timberwolves guard D'Angelo Russell and Hugo Boss, which had major success on social media. "It became at the time the number one most viewed and engaged with branded content post on Instagram ever," Mason said.[3] The video shows Russell, who left a photoshoot to play basketball on a court nearby. Russell takes the ball and ends up crossing over one of the defenders on him. The defender fell to the ground and the crowd went crazy. The video ended up with nearly four million views and 800,000 likes. "We shot it in a way that made it feel very organic to the platform. We shot it on a phone and kind of put the Snapchat caption in the bottom to make it look native," Mason said.[3] Incredible to see a branded content video have this much success since the audience usually picks up on sponsored content, but this looked like a regular iPhone video that anyone could shoot. I always thought the younger generations' eyes were used to picking up sponsored content on social media and would not engage like with an organic post. In this instance, I was wrong.

With Mason's help, B/R slowly started to flex their muscles after 2016 by creating unique branded content that made an impact on the sports social media space. B/R became more than just a media company but also a creative agency that could partner with any brand to create compelling content for the audience. Many brands will not just ask for content on B/R's social media channels but for the same content on their owned and operated channels. B/R has essentially extended their content offerings to brands. "We're getting more and more requests to function more like a hybrid creative agency/publisher, which is kind of our driving our strategy," Mason said.[3] More and more brands are coming to B/R not only for their ability to make great branded content but also to publish it on the company's social media, which has millions and millions of followers. B/R is essentially making money to create the branded content then getting paid by the brand to put that content on their accounts. Obviously, double the pay drives more revenue for B/R. I couldn't get the exact dollar amount, but I'm sure B/R makes millions per year from branded content. Mason has really grown the branded content department from the ground up by hiring the right people for the team and allowing them to let their creativity flourish on the business side.

In February 2019, B/R created Playmaker, the company's in-house creative services agency that partners with a sports team or other brand to create white label creative. "White label" refers to a fully supported product or service that's made by one company but sold by another.[4] Essentially B/R has continued to expand its capabilities to generate more and more revenue over time. Their business has evolved into not just supporting their company's content creation efforts but also support other brands, teams, and other organizations. I can't think of any other sports media organization that has created a creative services agency in-house. B/R continues to evolve as a business and stay ahead of the competition to stand out as one of the leaders in the sports media industry.

THE INS & OUTS TO MAKING MONEY ON SOCIAL MEDIA

At the end of the day, every business needs to make money to survive. Social media has slowly turned into a viable revenue generator for sports social media companies over the last five to seven years. Sports media companies don't just make money off advertisements, subscriptions, and other forms of revenue. There is a method to the madness, since the younger generations can detect ads on social media. You can't be overt with your ad placement. This is the main reason why sponsored content has taken a backseat to branded content. There should always be a delineation between the two. Some sports media organizations will go with sponsored content, and some will go with branded. Personally, I prefer branded content.

Overtime is a sports network focused on young sports fans founded in late 2016. They have done a great job of working with a bunch of the top brands in the industry. "We have produced branded content that makes sense for our audience," Head of content & operations, West Coast at Overtime Hunter Mandel told me that his company's sales team has figured out how to best navigate the branded content market. "The key is to just never sell out. The good thing about Overtime is our sales team and content team communicate very closely, and the sales team is not going to just execute a deal for the money. They're going to take it if it's right for us," he said.[5] Mandel hit the nail on the head. You shouldn't just take a deal because it's going to make the company money. Take the deal because it makes sense for your sports social media account's audience.

When you stray from your company's core values and don't play to the audience, you run the chance of losing them and pushing them toward your competitors. It's all about maintaining authenticity and not losing the connection to your audience. "If we take any deal we get and it's not good for the brand, then we're going to lose our audience, and we're going to lose our voice. What Overtime does great is we make money off branded and custom type content, but we maintain our voice," Mandel said.[5] As a major sports social media account that posts branded content, you need to maintain your voice because that's the lifeline between you and the audience. Some companies I've been at in the past have gotten comments from our following like "You're getting too corporate!" when we've post branded content that doesn't make sense with our audience's values. Your purpose when running a sports social media account is to connect to the audience. When you lose that, you lose the essence of what sports social media is all about. It's about being original, posting funny content, having authenticity, and thriving off your connection with the audience.

Will sports social media become more monetizable in the future? Yes, it will continue to grow. McGowan agreed with that statement when we discussed the future of monetization on social media. "I think over time it's going to become more of a vehicle to monetize, but then that's a fine line. I'm comforted by the fact that if we do it the right way, we have the right people, the right vision for it, then brands are going to want to be a part of it, he said."[1] As a sports social media account, you need to be in the best position to handle the future of monetization. If you're not ahead of the curve, you could start falling behind.

You have to continue understanding the consumption habits of your audience and future generations, so you can plan, organize, and attack how to gain a loyal following (instead of losing it) then keeping and growing that audience over time. Branded content is the key to generating revenue, but not all partnerships are best for the organization. You must be strategic and diligent with what deals you sign. Every sports social media wants and needs to make money, but at the end of the day, you have to be smart about what deals make the most sense for your organization and never underestimate the audience. They are smarter than you. I have certainly learned this during my career. It's okay to admit this because you serve the audience; they don't serve you.

CITATIONS:

1. Chris McGowan, Zoom call with author, February 10, 2021.

2. Ernie Santeralli, "Sponsored Content: What You Need To Know (And 9 Examples!)," *Activecampaign,* 2019, https://www.activecampaign.com/blog/sponsored-content.

3. Beckley Mason, in-person interview with author, June 19, 2019.

4. Drew Gainor, "Why A White Label Solution Is Easier Than Building Your Own," *Forbes,* Accessed February 13, 2021, https://www.forbes.com/sites/theyec/2014/06/03/why-a-white-label-solution-is-easier-than-building-your-own/?sh=2635a58edd9e.

5. Hunter Mandel, phone call with the author, December 10, 2020.

CHAPTER 9:
THE BLEACHER REPORT EFFECT

"It was so apparent that Bleacher Report was playing chess. We were so many moves ahead of everyone else," —former Bleacher Report deputy editor of the Social Moments team Joey Merkel[1]

Social media wasn't what Bleacher Report was known for until 2015, a whole ten years after the company was launched by four high school friends, David Finocchio, Alexander Freund, Bryan Goldberg, and Dave Nemetz. All four were classmates at Menlo School in Atherton, California.[2] The company's first office was in Menlo Park, CA in spring 2007.

Over the next four years (from 2007-2011), the sports media startup passed competitors Sports Illustrated and CBS Sports in traffic and raised $36 million,[3] a staggering amount in less than five years. Imagine starting a company with your high school buddies in 2005 and passing your major competitors who are longstanding media conglomerates. B/R had the secret recipe: Let sports fans (literally fans who sat in the "bleachers") write articles they wanted to write. The company nurtured these writers and made them better over time.

I started to follow Bleacher Report and read their articles in 2010 when my writing career began at Indiana University. I enjoyed the writing of Bleacher Report because it was very opinionated and engaging. Two years later, during my junior year at IU, I accepted a position at B/R as a sports media intern. Over the next four months, I would publish over eighty columns/articles, which garnered more than two hundred thousand reads. This was a monumental internship in my career because my writing got better thanks to B/R's editors and intern managers, and my writing was seen by a lot of people.

In the year that I started my internship, B/R was acquired by Turner Sports (a company I would work for three years later). In 2012, B/R was acquired by Turner Broadcasting System for $175 million.[4] One of the bigger acquisitions in the sports media history. The reasoning behind Turner's move was they "were attracted to Bleacher Report's fast growth to a leading marketplace position and a valued consumer destination," President of sales, distribution of Turner Broadcasting David Levy said.[5]

In 2011, Forbes wrote an article called "Who's Doing It Right? Bleacher Report Turns Knowing Fans Into Reporters."[6] A year after the acquisition in 2013, B/R decided to hire more prominent writers. B/R hired Mike Freeman from CBS Sports, Howard Beck from the New York Times, Ethan Skolnick from the Palm Beach Post, Kevin Ding from Orange County Register, and Jared Zwerling from ESPN.[7] All were writers from competitors, but with the acquisition came more money to put into their staff. These bold moves were bringing more attention to the company, going from "writers in the bleachers" to well-trained sports journalists.

I was brought on the team in October 2015 as one of the first ten hires to manage social media for the company. I landed the job because I worked at Turner Sports from 2014–2015, and one of my managers told me to talk to former VP of social media Doug Bernstein about a potential position. I landed a social media editor role and packed my bags in Atlanta (from Turner Sports) and moved to New York City (B/R's second office location).

B/R transitioned from a web traffic and app downloads company into a social media and content-first organization. "It was interesting to see the rise of social, and I think it was not just betting on social but being willing to pivot completely to social. I think that B/R has been good about evolving. Moving from SEO to newsletter to social to content to longer form video and shows," multimedia director at B/R Ishaan Mishra said.[9] B/R hired and nurtured in-house creatives that would end up changing the sports social media industry forever.

THE MEDIA LAB STARTED B/R'S SOCIAL MEDIA REVOLUTION

Before 2015 really changed things for B/R in social media, in-house creative people were cultivating a group to pass around ideas. Numerous people were hired for separate jobs, but at some point, a few of them came together to start what was called The Media Lab.

Each member of The Media Lab brought their own strengths to the table. Bennett Spector was the leader who gave the team an infrastructure. Mishra came from a background in NBA graphic design with a love of innovation and experimentation. The Malamut brothers had previous experience in animation and created Game of Zones, an award-winning animated parody of HBO's Game of Thrones featuring NBA players and coaches. Finally, Will Leivenberg was a great product manager that the team relied on for structure and tools to build out these experiments. These five were able to slowly put B/R on the map because of one-off projects that went viral for the company.

One prime example was when Frozen swept the nation and became a global phenomenon, The Media Lab created a parody version of the song, "Let It Go." The Malamut brothers came together along with Mishra to create the viral song, "Let It Tank." This version featured Kobe Bryant (RIP) who was voiced over by Garth Taylor singing about "tanking," an NBA-related phrase about losing on purpose to get a high draft pick. This animation started to show B/R flexing their creative muscles, which resulted in a viral post. Although it was only posted on YouTube, the video garnered 2.3 million views and over 24,000 likes. One of the top five most-watched YouTube videos for B/R at the time.

The Media Lab would later go on to create The Left Shark Shuffle (dedicated to Katy Perry's 2015 Super Bowl performance), a Wolf of Wall Street and Mortal Kombat head swap videos that switched one person's head with another, and more.

"I think B/R was probably one of the first companies to start using head swap technology. Even to this day, they are the people that have gotten it perfect, like down to an absolute science where they quickly understood that quality was always going to set them apart from their competitors," Merkel said.[1]

Nowadays, memes are all over the internet. A meme is an idea, behavior, style, or usage that spreads from person to person within a culture.[10] Even in 2015, B/R was already on that bandwagon. B/R was producing memes that would connect and engage sports fans across the country. "The speed of memes moves faster than the speed of content. So, when you're trying to compete with the crowd, you're going to fail. That's why you have to lean into it," Mishra said.[9] B/R's Media Lab became very good at creating memes that helped change the company's reputation from SEO/website traffic to social media frontrunners in the sports world.

THE EMERGENCE OF THE SOCIAL MOMENTS TEAM

When the higher-ups at B/R started to see this success, they wanted to amplify and build a brand-new team dedicated to making viral memes that would put the company on the map for sports social media. It all began with The Media Lab, but the evolution of that team would flip the sports social media world on its head.

"I think it was decided that this is something that we should be doing full-time. It has the potential to be big enough that it shouldn't just be a handful of people doing this as a side project; it should be a handful of people who should be doing this full-time. They should be creators," Merkel said.[1]

In the fall of 2015 (just two years after the birth of The Media Lab), B/R created the Original Social Content team to continue to be innovative in the sports social media space. The Media Lab transformed into a two-person team led by Merkel and Spencer Oshman. Merkel told me a story about how they created a meme animation/song called "Hotline Zing," which featured then Knicks big man Kristaps Porzingis mixed with the Drake song "Hotline Bling." Porzingis was dancing in the B/R meme similar to Drake in his music video. The video was quote-tweeted by Porzingis and recorded over two hundred thousand views on B/R's YouTube channel. This was just one moment where the Original Social Content team was allowed to flex their creative muscles, and it paid off.

Later on in 2016, the Original Social Content team was renamed the Social Moments team. B/R hired a bunch of new creators and ideators (both terms we used at B/R) for that team. "By January 2016, we had full-time editors, full-time writers, and full-time graphic designers. They kept building out this team," Merkel said.[1] Merkel explained that leadership selected people from the Social Programming team as well. This team was becoming a priority for B/R when most sports media companies didn't have a social creative team within the company. "B/R just really got so far ahead of the game," Merkel said.[1]

The Social Moments team became the gold standard for sports social media and was known for many viral posts from B/R: memes to high-end videos to jersey swaps to quote graphics to animations to motion effects videos and more. I'm not saying there was a viral post every day, but there would be numerous ones each month. "They didn't always hit, but it wasn't always about the virality. It was also about the partnerships," Merkel said.[1]

The Social Moments team created some amazing moments in sports social media history on top of the partnerships they were building on the side. One of the main ideators of the Social Moments team was CJ Toledano. Toledano was brought on the team because of his background with stand-up comedy and creating viral moments for the Detroit Pistons. Toledano talked to me about numerous viral moments he was a part of, but two stood out. The Cubs winning the World Series over the Cleveland Indians meme and a rom-com trailer named Chasing Larry.

In the 2016 World Series, the Cubs were down three games to one in a seven-game series. If the Cubs were to lose one more game, they would lose the World Series. Amazingly, the Cubs won the next three games in a row to win their first World Series title since 1908. Before the seventh game of the series, the Social Moments team thought of a five-second video meme that would be posted if the Cubs won. The Cubs won, and B/R posted one of their most viral memes ever. It was a simple video that said "Cleveland Blew a 3-1 Lead" on the famous Wrigley Field Marquee (where the Cubs play) with fans on the street cheering. I was fascinated by the meme and decided to calculate the numbers on Facebook, Twitter, and Instagram. The five-second video totaled over 6 million views and over 350,000 interactions (likes, comments, retweets, and quote tweets) on those three platforms. It was only five seconds long! But it was posted at the perfect time, and sports fans around the world loved every second of it.

"We dropped it when the Cubs won, and I think it got like 70,000 retweets, which was just unheard of to us back then," Toledano said. [11]

One of my favorite moments in sports social media history (yes, I'm biased) was the rom-com trailer, Chasing Larry. Before the 2017 NBA Finals, the Social Moments team made this meme trailer named after the Larry O'Brien Championship trophy. CJ told me about his thought process to create the viral meme trailer:

"We always get these NBA Finals trailers that are kind of motivational, tight, energetic in a black and white cinematic. I thought, 'What if we showed it in a different framing? Show it in a totally opposite tone than it's ever been shown.' And I was like, 'Let's show it as a rom-com. Two guys are fighting over not a girl but a trophy, and all the drama that is happening on both sides,'" Toledano said.[11]

Toledano said that "Chasing Larry took off."[11] The 1-minute, 28-second video received nearly 4 million views and over 400,000 interactions across Facebook, Instagram, Twitter, and YouTube.[12] I'm sure if you're a diehard sports social media fan, you remember both of these posts. At Bleacher Report, it was more than about just going viral; it was about the impact we were making on sports fans around the world. Although we recognized the other sports media outlets we were competing with, it was more of a competition within the office to keep getting better and better on social. "One of the great things about being on an all-star team is being willing to talk to each other about how you can get better. Steel sharpens steel. We were all trying to sharpen each other. We were all trying to challenge each other," Mishra said.[9]

THE IMPACT OF THE MALAMUT BROTHERS

If you ask any fan of B/R over the years, they will likely tell you they love the sports media company for numerous reasons, but two that usually come up are the memes and "Game of Zones." In case you didn't know, the series lasted six years and totaled seven seasons and thirty-nine episodes. The series garnered 120 Million views on YouTube alone! Pretty remarkable because this was the brainchild of Adam and Craig Malamut, two brothers and longtime NBA fans who turned their passion for Game of Thrones and pop culture into a sports culture phenomenon.

"I think the hiring of the Malamuts shows how important it is to give intelligent people a chance to tell their story," Mishra said.[9] The back story on how these brothers landed at B/R is pretty impressive. Adam is a writer/producer who taught himself animation using Lynda.com courses. Adam had a long stint in the TV space in Los Angeles doing all kinds of jobs like producer and writer until he landed at B/R. Craig has a Master's degree in astronomy and astrophysics but also was a cartoon artist growing up. He told me that he stopped before getting his PHD to join Adam in Los Angeles to learn how to animate.

Adam and Craig's first animated show together was 'Sports Friends' on Yahoo Screen. These series was noticed by Spector, who brought the brothers in to talk. "Bennett came to us, had seen Basketball Friends, Sports Friends and he was a fan. Bennett wanted to work with us, so we pitched a menu of ideas and one of them was *Game of Zones*. So we made the first episode, and it went viral," Adam said.[13] The first episode hit 8.2 million views on YouTube, which is still the most in Game of Zones history and an all-time top ten video in views for B/R. "What we didn't expect was how well it would do, and the fact that Bennett would be like, 'Do you guys want to come in-house after that?'" Adam said.[13]

The idea of Game of Zones came from the brothers' love of Game of Thrones and them wanting to do something more sports-related in the animation world. The brothers would make connections from the NBA world to the Game of Thrones world, which fans of both could pick up on. "LeBron was Jamie, and Derrick Rose was Bran, and the Spurs were the White Walkers," Craig said.[14]

The brothers' work was heavily praised throughout B/R. "The Malamuts are everything to Game of Zones. It's their brainchild. They wrote it, animated it (for the first season), voiced it. Adam and Craig are immensely talented individuals who have a brilliant sense of comedy," Bernstein said.[8]

The number of episodes per series would grow year after year. Season one was two episodes, seasons two and three were three episodes each, then seasons four through six were at least eight episodes each. Season seven (the final season) was five episodes, including a twelve-minute series finale called "The GOAT." Most episodes were three to eight minutes long.

Not only did the episodes grow, but the staff grew too. The show started with the brothers, then grew to seven, and then finally fifteen people in the last three seasons. The series was even sponsored by McDonalds and State Farm at different points. It was amazing to be in the same building as these two creative sports wizards who turned their love of basketball and Game of Thrones into a game-changing moment for B/R. I was honored when I had the chance to post Game of Zones to any B/R social media accounts because I knew the hard work it took to create this content. And I knew the episodes would get tons and tons of views each time. No episode ever got under 1.6 million views on YouTube.[13]

Adam and Craig not only changed the culture at B/R but were also a sports social media phenomenon that has yet to be and might never be replicated. While I'm sad the show is over, I know the brothers will move on to do great things in this "content-focused world" we live in. As Bernstein said about the brothers, "Their ability to combine their comedic sensibilities with sports is unparalleled."[8]

B/R has had many moments throughout its sixteen-year history to be proud of, from the creation of The Media Lab to the evolution of the Social Moments team to the disruption created in the sports social media world by the Malamut brothers. But mostly the company should be proud of the amazing work the people did in the office. I'm proud to say that I was a part of B/R's history in making them one of the top sports media companies in the world.

CITATIONS:

1. Joey Merkel, phone call with the author, January 22, 2021.

2. "Menlo School: News » News Detail," Web.Archive,.Org. Accessed January 30. 2021, https://web.archive.org/web/20090801034239/http://www.menloschool.org/news/detail.aspx?pageaction=ViewSinglePublic&LinkID=2069&ModuleID=35.

3. Sarah Lacy, 2011. "As Football Season Kicks Off, Bleacher Report Raises $22 Million More," Techcrunch, https://techcrunch.com/2011/08/24/as-football-season-kicks-off-bleacher-report-raises-22-million-more/.

4. Jeff Bercovici, "Turner Buys Bleacher Report, Next-Gen Sports Site, For $175M-Plus," Forbes, 2012, https://www.forbes.com/sites/jeffbercovici/2012/08/06/turner-buys-bleacher-report-next-gen-sports-site-for-175m-plus/?sh=507e68e7843d.

5. Ingrid Lunden, "Update: It's Done. Time Warner Buys Bleacher Report, Price Reportedly $175M," Techcrunch, 2012, https://techcrunch.com/2012/08/06/time-warnerbleacher-report-deal-gets-ftc-nod-price-reportedly-under-200/.

6. Lewis DVorkin, "Who's Doing It Right? Bleacher Report Turns Knowing Fans Into Reporters," *Forbes,* 2011, https://www.forbes.com/sites/lewisdvorkin/2011/08/22/whos-doing-it-right-bleacher-report-turns-knowing-fans-into-reporters/?sh=12a82b85ddba.

7. Ed Sherman, "Bleacher Report Adds Howard Beck; Expected To Go After More Writers With Big-Money Offers," *Shermanreport,* 2013, http://www.shermanreport.com/bleacher-report-adds-howard-beck-expected-to-go-after-more-writers-with-big-money-offers/.

8. Doug Bernstein, email message to author, January 29, 2021.

9. Ishaan Mishra, phone call with author, January 29, 2021.

10. Merriam-Webster, s.v. "meme (n.)," accessed January 31, 2021, https://www.merriam-webster.com/dictionary/meme.

11. CJ Toledano, phone call with author, December 23, 2020.

12. Analytical Information from CrowdTangle and research on platform insights.

13. Adam Malamut, in-person interview, June 24, 2019.

14. Craig Malamut, in-person interview, June 24, 2019.

CHAPTER 10:
THE UNLIKELY RISE OF HOUSE OF HIGHLIGHTS

The numbers: 27 million Instagram followers. 10 million TikTok followers. 3 million YouTube subscribers. Over 200,000 Twitter followers. 26,000 Facebook likes. If you do the math, that's over 40 million followers!

This is not ESPN, Bleacher Report, FOX Sports, or Barstool Sports. It's *House of Highlights (HoH)*, a media brand that has taken the sports social media world by storm. Beloved by GenZ and millennial sports fans around the world, it's an account that started with zero Instagram followers like the rest of us but has had a monumental rise to stardom. The fact that I'm writing a whole chapter about HoH couldn't have been conceived six years ago. Not because I didn't believe in the HoH brand but because Omar was a one-man show competing against longstanding sports media brands.

Omar's story is one of dedication, perseverance, and an unmatched work ethic in the sports social media space. This is the story of how Omar Raja became Omar and grew one of the largest Instagram accounts in sports social media history.

THE BACKSTORY OF HOUSE OF HIGHLIGHTS

Before House of Highlights became what it is today, Omar's social media journey started at an early age. In 2006, twelve-year-old Omar wanted a PlayStation 3. His dad said that he wasn't going to pay $600 for the console. So he made his dad a deal: let's split it 50/50. Making $300 as a twelve-year-old isn't easy. Omar said, "I had no idea how to do that."[1] Omar soon figured out a way to make the money. He washed his neighbor's cars then decided to go the digital route. He made a gaming website called "UnrealGamers.net."[1] He advertised the website on the official PlayStation forums and ended up making a couple hundred bucks. Omar had the light-bulb moment: "Oh, there's a way to make money off the internet."[1] Omar ended up getting his PlayStation 3 and continued to post content on his gaming website to make money.

Don't forget, this is a twelve-year-old. But the story doesn't end there. Two years later, he started making YouTube videos for Machinima Inc., a multi-platform online entertainment company started in 2000.[2] Omar started a reoccurring content series called The Top Seven Luckiest Call of Duty Plays."[1] These would allow gamers to email Omar videos, and Omar would video edit this segment for Machinima to post online. This started from when Omar was fourteen and lasted through college when he needed some extra money. On top of this, Omar was making YouTube accounts, but "they never really blew up, he said"[1]

At some point during his freshman year at the University of Central Florida, Omar decided to switch up his love for YouTube onto Instagram. "I'll never forget. I told one of my friends that I was going to make a big Instagram page. We were watching a big ESPN game, I believe Heat-Clippers, and he kind of just chuckled." Omar went on to prove his friend wrong and started his passion for Instagram with his first account called "SportsPosters" in 2013. Omar would design NBA graphics on Photoshop for people to use as iPhone wallpaper. At the time, video was a part of Instagram, so graphics were his way to build an audience. He also reposted other designers' graphics from around the world. Omar said the account hit "300,000 or 400,000 followers" at its peak.

Omar noticed a trend during 2014 that video accounts were growing as the platform evolved. Before Omar created HoH, he created FilthiestCrossovers. "It was crossover clips, ankle-breaker clips."[1] Omar nonchalantly said to me, "It got to a million."[1] The work ethic Omar was putting in is outstanding to me. While I was starting my first social media job at Turner Sports, he was slowly building a sports social media empire behind the scenes.

Later in 2014, Omar decided to create his third Instagram account, HoH. This would include all kinds of sports videos, not just NBA highlights, and UGC from all around the world, all submitted through the Instagram direct messages. That account was started because Omar is a big Miami Heat fan who grew up just twenty miles from the American Airlines Arena. In June 2014, LeBron James opted out of his contract and left the Heat to return to the Cleveland Cavaliers. That moment struck a chord with Omar. He missed LeBron and the championship Heat teams. To show his love for those teams, Omar would search YouTube and other social media platforms to share memories with his friends.[3]

Just as the Heat had their Big Three (LeBron, Dwyane Wade, and Chris Bosh), so did Omar on Instagram (SportsPosters, FilthiestCrossovers, and HoH). "It was pretty clear that House of Highlights was the LeBron of that group. I personally had more fun because it required me to watch every single game instead of sit in photoshop for an hour and mess around photos," Omar said in a Sportstechie article.[4] Video took over the Instagram world and Omar's activity on the platform. Omar consumed content like no other person in sports social media. Watching every single NBA game and looking for those magic moments that his audience would love. He can vividly recall past videos of LeBron yelling at Heat teammate Mario Chalmers and Wade throwing Mike Bibby's shoe into the first row during a game. "Those were like the early moments I would take advantage of," Omar said.[1] Moments like these are what grew HoH from zero followers nearly half a million followers in less than a year.

There was moment where Omar knew HoH was going to be something special. "I think when I knew how fast I got to 500K, saying to myself 'What in the world is going on here?' Then I saw Snoop Dogg followed the account," he said.[1] Those two milestones are what really touched Omar and showed him he was on track to building a great IG account with a huge following.

In mid-2015, Omar's HoH account garnered the attention of B/R. Former VP of social media Doug Bernstein reached out to Omar about the potential of working together. The first discussion between Bernstein and Omar was very casual. "I sent him an email. I said, 'Hey, this is Doug. I work for Bleacher Report. I'd love to talk to you about how we could work together.' He responded, 'What do you want?' and then said, 'All right, when do you want to get on the phone?'"[5]

Bernstein said that conversation didn't last long because Omar was eyeing NBA free agency at the time. NBA free agency is the time where free agents are allowed to sign with new teams. Omar found out that Kevin Love was re-signing with the Cavaliers[6] and hung up on "the VP of social. I thought about it, and I was like, 'I like that. Because he's dedicated to the account. He's going to put that before any type of opportunity, and that's the type of person that you want to work with,'" Bernstein said.[5]

A few months after their first call in October 2015, Omar was thinking about whether or not to allow B/R to acquire his business, then something unusual happened. "I was even like, 'God, give me a sign!' And then two days later, the House of Highlights account got hacked," he said.[1] At that point, Omar felt his life was ruined, even recalling the exact day and time it happened in our conversation. Thirteen days later, Bernstein saved the day and got Omar's account back by emailing different people at Facebook. Two months after HoH got hacked, B/R acquired the account, which had a bit over one million followers at the time.

Why did B/R make the move to acquire HoH and give Omar his first job out of college? Bernstein was impressed with Omar on multiple levels. "The macro reason was we always saw ourselves at B/R as the disruptor in the space, the challenger brand. After about 10 years or so, we were starting to become more established. If anybody was going to disrupt us, we wanted it to be ourselves. We saw House of Highlights as the biggest potential challenger to Bleacher Report for a younger audience, Bernstein said.[5]

Other reasons include it was Omar's voice and captioning abilities on social. "He had a very distinct voice. So the way Omar captioned, I just really liked it. It was extremely relatable. It was a way how like friends texted each other. It just like was a very distinct first-person voice that I hadn't seen anything like that before," Bernstein said.[5] Second, Bernstein liked Omar's content selection for his account. "Omar has an incredible eye for content, and you saw that even in 2014, 2015. He was finding user-generated content videos that our team of eight people wasn't finding. Also, he would find those little moments in the NBA that everybody would miss," Bernstein said.[5] Finally, the eye-catching analytics of HoH stood out to Bernstein. "The rate of growth that House of Highlights was posting was truly remarkable. Then the engagement rate was really high," Bernstein said.[5]

Omar's work ethic stood out to Bernstein. "Not that many twenty-year-olds are going to make sure they're posting four or five NBA highlights every night. So I think its persistence and dedication, and you see the growth of the account, and you say there's something to build here," Bernstein said.[5]

Omar not only had his first job out of college at one of the top sports media outlets but was allowed to run his account that he started a little over a year before. What was the plan of attack now that Omar's part of the media conglomerate Turner Sports (which acquired Bleacher Report in 2012)?[7] Simple, let Omar be Omar.

THE EYE-POPPING GROWTH OF HOH

Bernstein explained that the B/R leadership team just wanted "him to do what he does best. Just go and grow it. Let Omar take that organic growth and run with it. He did a tremendous job with that."[5] By January 2016,

HoH had 2.1 million followers, and over a year later in March 2017, the account had over 5 million followers. The Instagram account went from about five hundred thousand in July 2015 to over five million by March 2017! Less than two years later, it grew ten times the size.[8] Earlier in 2021, the account became the first US sports media brand to surpass 25 million followers on Instagram.

Omar didn't gain popularity in the public eye for running House of Highlights until in 2017. It all started with Bleacher Report employee CJ Toledano writing "Nice caption Omar" in the comments of one of HoH's posts. The buzz started building: Who was running this account? Who was Omar? As Bernstein said, "Who is the man behind the myth, the legend?"[5] So starting out in 2018, B/R made the decision to make Omar a "front-facing talent."[5] This led to more publicity opportunities for Omar including a *Fast Company* article calling Omar "a twenty-three-year-old Instagram savant" as the account hit ten million Instagram followers. Fast Company is a monthly American business magazine published in print and online that focuses on technology, business, and design.[9] After articles from Fast Company, Esquire, and Sports Illustrated were published, Omar started to get recognized on the street during his walk from his apartment to the office.

In late 2017, Doug and the higher-ups at B/R made the decision to grow the HoH team because of the opportunity to evolve the IG account. "We don't want it to be just an Instagram account. We want it to be a brand, and we want it to be a business. I think as part of building a business, you kind of naturally have to evolve and grow the team," Bernstein said.[5]

Bernstein's title changed to General Manager of HoH in early 2018. B/R moved Drew Corrigan from the Social Moments team to being Omar's first team member at HoH. Omar and Corrigan ran the account together for a year before the B/R higher-ups decided to grow it more. Three more programmers (people who curate content to post on the account) were hired to help Omar and Corrigan run the account.

I was a senior programmer for B/R for over two years. I would find content for our social media accounts, and if I found videos that resonated more with the House of Highlights audience, I would them send over to Omar and Drew. B/R and HoH have different audiences; B/R was more millennial, and HoH was more for the Gen Z audience. Although both accounts were run under the same roof in New York City, we posted different things depending on what the audience wanted.

UGC and NBA highlights weren't the only thing HoH was posting. The account evolved into doing more original content and branded content. "We not only need to curate content, but we also need to start creating our own content. We needed to have production resources to support branded content," Bernstein said.[5] HoH got a Twitter show sponsored by McDonald's, which was hosted by Omar and Toledano. "It's a great evolution for the page to go from an Instagram account to having a show. I definitely was excited about it," Omar said.[1] Omar has always been a fan of McDonald's and finally got the opportunity to have a show sponsored by them. "I would eat McDonald's every other day. That was the 'we made it' moment," he said.[1]

"I'm noticing that some brands and some companies are relying too heavily on the aggregation and the curation of content and forgetting the part where they need to make something themselves. Something like House of Highlights was a highlight aggregator, and then they were able to turn that brand to create original series," Braband said.[11]

Not just curating content but creating original content has been noticed by competitors in the sports social media space.

In mid-2019, HoH became the only US sports media brand to surpass ESPN across social media platforms with over twelve million Instagram followers, another incredible milestone for the HoH brand. As Omar said a few months later on Twitter, "Went from 0 followers to 15,000,000 and officially became the most followed US Sports Media account on Instagram! 5 years have flown by!"[13] Omar couldn't have said it any better. The evolution of HoH is incredible and deserves a whole chapter in a book about sports social media.

HoH all started because one twenty-year-old college student wanted to reminisce about old Heat championship teams after LeBron left Miami. The General Manager of HoH later explained how the team has grown to over twenty people. Omar launched the account in mid-2014, and in 2021, the brand employs over twenty people and makes a significant amount of money from branded content.

"When I got the opportunity to work at House of Highlights, it was the most exciting thing. To just see the page evolve, for it to be starting out as an NBA-centric account and grow into something so much more, being this youth culture media brand, is rewarding," Director of Programming at HoH Caroline Jastremski said.[14]

OMAR'S SIGNIFICANT MOVE TO ESPN

PHOTO BY MELISSA RAWLINS / ESPN IMAGES

Omar's story doesn't stop at HoH. In 2020, ESPN announced that Omar would be moving to ESPN from HoH to increase their social media presence. Omar will serve as the main voice of ESPN's "SportsCenter" Instagram account, which had 17.2 million followers then and now has over 25 million. The SportsCenter Instagram bio literally starts off by saying "I'm @Omar and this is SportsCenter."

Amazing to see a twenty-year-old running perhaps the top sports Instagram account in the world. Omar has interviewed Dwyane Wade, Stephen Curry, and Damian Lillard among other NBA players during his seven-year career in sports social media. Not to mention the automatically eye-stopping job title of Founder of House of Highlights. His resume will always include that IG account started with zero followers and now has over twenty-three million.

What a journey by Omar, a truly amazing example of working hard, staying persistent, and always growing year after year. Everyone in social media (not just sports social media) should appreciate his rise to stardom and his story of success. "I kind of look back at the journey and say, 'How in the world did we get here?'" Omar said.[1] We got here because Omar had all the qualities you need to succeed. Omar will always be one of the true game changers of the sports social media industry. When asked what he is most proud of with HoH, he says that the account survived. The account not only survived, but it also thrived in a competitive sports social media landscape.

CITATIONS:

1. Omar Raja, phone call with author, February 3, 2021.

2. Wikipedia; Wikipedia's "Machinima, Inc." entry. Accessed 2021. https://en.wikipedia.org/wiki/Machinima,_Inc.

3. Cale Guthrie Weissman, "Bleacher Report's Secret Weapon Is A 23-Year-Old Instagram Savant," *Fast Company,* 2018, https://www.fastcompany.com/40519104/bleacher-reports-secret-weapon-is-a-23-year-old-instagram-savant.

4. Joe Lemire, "The Inside Story Of How House of Highlights Scored 10 Million Instagram Followers," *Sporttechie,* 2018, https://www.sporttechie.com/bleacher-report-house-of-highlights-omar-raja-10-million-instagram/.

5. Doug Bernstein, in-person interview with author, November 27, 2020.

6. "Cavaliers Re-Sign Forward Kevin Love | Cleveland Cavaliers,". Cleveland Cavaliers, 2015, https://www.nba.com/cavaliers/releases/love-signing-150709.

7. Jeff Bercovici, "Turner Buys Bleacher Report, Next-Gen Sports Site, For $175M-Plus," Forbes, 2012, https://www.forbes.com/sites/jeffbercovici/2012/08/06/turner-buys-bleacher-report-next-gen-sports-site-for-175m-plus/?sh=5a51b6977843.

8. Paul Sarconi, "Why Instagram Is Suddenly The Place For Sports Highlights," Wired, 2017, https://www.wired.com/2017/03/instagram-sports-highlights/.

9. Wikipedia; Wikipedia's "Fast Company" entry; 2021. https://en.wikipedia.org/wiki/Fast_Company.

10. Laia Cardona, "What Is Branded Content? Definition, Advantages And Examples," *Cyberclick*, 2020, https://www.cyberclick.net/numericalblogen/what-is-branded-content-definition-advantages-and-examples.

11. Steve Braband, phone interview with author, January 19, 2021.

12. Wikipedia; Wikipedia's "DAZN" entry; Accessed February 8, 2021, https://en.wikipedia.org/wiki/DAZN.

13. Omar Raja (@OmarESPN) Twitter, November 26, 2019.

14. Caroline Jastremski, phone interview with author, November 24, 2020.

CHAPTER 11:

SPORTS SOCIAL MEDIA ISN'T ALL FUN AND GAMES

"Social media has it's positives and negatives. It all comes down to if you're mature enough to use it or have knowledge on its consequences, because once you hit that button, you can't retract that statement."
—Zyad Ismael[1]

Social media is not always fun and games. People go down a dark hole of depression, there is harassment, and bullying just for being different or not running with the popular crowd. Sports social media is no different. Because anyone can use any social media platform, it opens up the vicious cycle of trolling, especially in sports. A troll is not only a dwarf under a bridge but also "a person who intentionally antagonizes others online by posting inflammatory, irrelevant, or offensive comments or other disruptive content."[2] When an athlete performs badly or a tweet is deleted, someone takes a screenshot. Whether you're an athlete or social media manager, you leave yourself open to attack because you are in the public eye.

"Now you can just type in your name on Twitter, and you can have some 12-year-old saying you didn't play well and you're not worth your contract, so that is definitely the downside of it. It's a positive in how much direct access you get to your fans and how you can control your brand and message. It's a negative when you have fans who are trolling you or doing anything nefarious," Vice President, NBA Player Marketing & Business Development at Catalyst Sports Brandon Curran said.[3] Curran told me that times have changed for an athlete from a big media organization commenting negatively toward your performance to now the public saying anything they want about you. "They have to deal with trolls, so there is definitely a mental aspect to it. It is a lot more challenging, that athletes didn't have to previously go through, because in the past you may see you are only getting criticized on ESPN or in the local newspaper." he said.[3]

Not only are athletes trolled on social media, but social media managers take harassment too. I didn't sign up to take my first job in social media with Turner Sports for the chance to be trolled or demeaned. But it has happened to me, teaching me to have thick skin in this industry. The audience is ruthless and waiting for you to mess up, so they can jump all over you in the replies of the tweet. There were two instances I will always remember from my time at Turner Sports.

The first was a birthday tweet where I spelled Muggsy Bogues's name wrong. I scheduled the tweet the night before, thinking nothing of it. We used a program called Spredfast where you could schedule Facebook posts and tweets. I misspelled his name by writing "Mugsy" and not "Muggsy." My coworker deleted the tweet about seven or eight minutes after the tweet was posted, but that was enough time for the audience to screenshot it. We sent out a new tweet with the correct spelling of Muggsy's name, but the audience replied to the new tweet with screenshots of the tweet with the misspelling, jumping all over me. I heard the disappointment from my manager, but she also told me this was a learning experience and to double-check the name on Google next time. I have always double-checked names since that tweet.

It was a hard lesson, but I soon learned things could be much worse. The second moment was when I tweeted out a video of former Wizards guard John Wall throwing up gang signs to the Atlanta Hawks crowd in the middle of a game. Personally, I thought the video showed Wall bringing the energy to the road arena, but our followers didn't seem to agree. Once again, fans screenshotted the tweet and replied with it repeatedly on our next few tweets. My manager and I decided to delete the tweet, but the damage was done. My manager made me write an email to the Turner Sports PR team telling them what the tweet was, why we deleted it, and to not be surprised if we received negative publicity over it. I was frightened. I felt the room shaking and believed that might have been my last tweet with Turner Sports. I went to the bathroom and called my mom crying, telling her what had happened. Thankfully she calmed me down and told me "it's not the end of the world," as she has on numerous occasions where I've made mistakes. And she was right: Turner Sports didn't receive bad publicity over it, and my job was still safe. Things could've been much worse, and I'm thankful they weren't.

Former social media coordinator at the Golden State Warriors Julie Phayer received much worse treatment than I ever have all because of her gender. For nearly six years, Phayer was the voice of the Warriors, one of the best franchises in the NBA that won three titles during her time with the organization. Even though the team was winning, and she was one of the top social media employees in the NBA, there was vicious harassment happening behind the scenes. People direct messaged Phayer saying that "they hope the entire team rapes her" and that "she bleeds to death."[4] Phayer received numerous death threats and constant messages about the "sexualization of women," trolls saying that "she must be screwing the players."[4] Phayer's story is a microcosm of the harassment that women who work in sports get on a daily basis.

●○○○○ T-Mobile 📶 ❄️   8:51 PM   77% 🔋⚡

Messages

WTF @JoseBoatcrash   7s
Nigger

♡ @Chris_Orioles   5m
💯

⚽ @soshnigod   5m
💯

Cleon @g0odexecution   14m
i hope the whole warriors team rapes your bones
u ugly bitch, then the warriors team gets nuked...

Joey @JoeyCliffy   14m
You single by any chance?

Suspended @hanksprilla_   14m
Fuck you whore.

Chris @Murtinez97   14m
Hey

mlu @mshwnlychurslf   18m
Get cancer I hope Draymond forcefully rips you
in half with his cock

🏠 Home   🔍 Explore   🔔 Notifications   ✉️ Messages   👤 Me

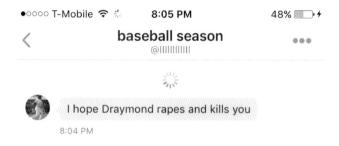

(Photos from Julie Phayer's Twitter Account/Direct Messages)

On top of the harassment she received, the Warriors organization didn't give her the support she needed when she told them about numerous incidents. The human resources team didn't provide professional help even after she told them about the stress it was causing on her mental health. In fact, she was reprimanded by the organization in her yearly reviews for taking mental health days over the hateful messages she received. The interview with Phayer both shocked me about the attacks that trolls can do to social media managers, but also the lack of support from a well-respected championship organization.

It's an awful part of sports that doesn't get written about or amplified in the news. Phayer should never have been treated that way. Hopefully, one day we can end this vicious cycle. I was shocked to hear Phayer's story because men in sports social media usually get the "intern must have posted that" comment, but she has opened my eyes and shown me the dark side of sports social media.

CHAD SHANKS' INFAMOUS HOUSTON ROCKETS TWEET

Something I will always remember is what the Houston Rockets tweeted after the team defeated the Dallas Mavericks during the first round of the 2015 NBA playoffs. At the time, I was working for Turner Sports and covering NBA TV and NBA on TNT social media. The tweet had two emojis, the horse emoji and the gun emoji, with words saying, "Shhhhh. Just close your eyes. It will all be over soon." After seeing that tweet from my Atlanta desk, I chuckled a bit and thought immediately that the social media manager in charge of the tweet would most likely be fired. Chad Shanks, the man behind that tweet, was fired the next day, but I caught up with him and learned the full story six years later.

Shanks said that at first, social media was seen as a joke in the Rockets organization in the early 2010s. The CEO of the team would laugh after the manager of their social media team would go over the analytics. He just didn't see the importance of it. Eventually the CEO opened up to social media and the impact it could make on their organization. Shanks used to do email marketing and web content for the team, then he was asked to handle the team's social media accounts. After a few months with the new role, Shanks developed an account that could "have its own personality. It [could] take on that persona as the voice of the fans."[5]

Of that infamous day, Shanks said "parts of it were a blur and parts he can remember vividly."[5] He went to the arena, and it appeared to be just another day covering the Rockets. He typed out the tweet, showed it to another social media employee, and it went out. The idea was the Mavericks were an older team and "when an aging player was liking taking a horse to pasture," he said.[5] Shanks didn't think the tweet would be interpreted the way people did, and he said that was his biggest mistake. He thought the audience would see it at a playful joke, but most people didn't take it lightly.

The tweet went out and immediately his boss said, "What the hell was that with the gun?" Shanks said.[5] The two went to one of the higher-ups of the organization to discuss what to do, and he said to delete it. After deleting the tweet, it had a life of its own where it went viral for all the wrong reasons, and NBA fans around the world passed around the screenshot like a game of hot potato.

The next day, Shanks got to the office and immediately had a meeting with HR and his boss. They said they were terminating his employment and ushered him out of the building without explanation. As he was driving home, he called his wife to tell her he was just fired which he called, "the worst moment in my life."[5] Shanks later tweeted, "Sometimes you can go too far. I will no longer run the @HoustonRockets but am grateful to the organization that let me develop an online voice."[6] The infamous tweet turned into national and international news. "I started getting calls from people I knew in the media. Even local media started showing up to my doorstep," he said.[5]

That wasn't the end of the story. A childhood neighbor messaged him on Facebook saying that he saw the news in Australia. Days after the firing, Shanks was ostracized from the Rockets organization. Department heads from the team told their employees to not talk or text Shanks. "I was persona non grata."[5] It's not easy going from an organization where you worked for over three years, enduring late nights and working weekends and holidays with fellow coworkers, to being denied communication with them.

Shanks saw the transformation of the Rockets social media during his three years there. "I got to see it grow from a literal laughingstock within the organization to I could do whatever the hell I wanted, and no one really seemed to pay attention to the point one night of something that I tweeted became literally international news," he said.[5] Shanks ended up getting a job a few months later. Shanks's infamous tweet wasn't just a learning lesson for Shanks, but for me and many others. Watch what you tweet and double-check with the higher-ups if you're unsure about the post. Shanks has lived past this moment and sustained a successful career in social media.

LAREMY TUNSIL'S BONG PHOTO BEFORE THE 2016 NFL DRAFT

The NFL draft is an event where dreams come true for more than 250 players, the dream of being selected by one of the thirty-two teams in the league. In 2016, Laremy Tunsil was one of the projected top picks of the draft. USA Today's mock draft projected Tunsil to go No. 1 overall that year.[7] In a mock draft, journalists predict how they think the draft will turn out, going team by team and selecting a player for each team's first-round picks. Tunsil was the superstar of the draft, and all the media members and teams believed it. Ten minutes before the draft began, a video was tweeted from Tunsil's Twitter account that showed him smoking from a gas-mask bong. The timing couldn't have been worse. The tweet was deleted, but the harm was already done. This tweet was national news with articles from ESPN, the New York Times, the Washington Post, and numerous other media outlets.

Tunsil ended up getting drafted No. 13 overall by the Miami Dolphins. After the draft was done, Tunsil told ESPN that he was "blessed" to be selected by the Dolphins and "we're trying to find out who hacked the account."[8] As the possible No. 1 pick overall, Tunsil would have made a reported $28.65 million for his first contract. With the drop to No. 13, he ended up making $12.76 million.[9] If you do the math, that's nearly $16 million lost over the four-year contract. Teams were afraid to select Tunsil because of the incident, which dropped his selection in the draft. The Washington Post wrote a whole story entitled, "Who hacked Laremy Tunsil?" "Dolphins believe it was former financial advisory of Laremy Tunsil who leaked the gas-mask video, according to a source."[10] The former financial advisor was fired by Tunsil before the draft. You clearly have to watch who you trust when you are in the public eye.

Tunsil's infamous bong photo will be remembered by the sports social media community and must have frightened him at the time. Imagine being in his shoes, thinking he was going to be the No. 1 pick in the draft to dropping twelve spots because of damaging bong photo. Luckily, Tunsil is having a great career in the league and has made the Pro Bowl twice in his career (2019 and 2020). In 2020, Tunsil ended up signing a three-year, $66 million contract with the Houston Texans.[11] While the incident might be behind Tunsil, it still is a moment he will never forget.

KEVIN DURANT'S MULTIPLE TWITTER ACCOUNTS

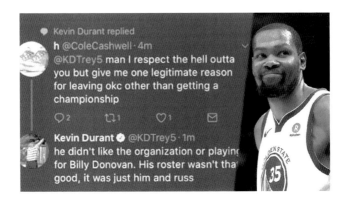

Kevin Durant (KD) is known as one of the top five players in the NBA for the last several years. He is globally known for his 6'10" size, incredible shooting ability, and championship pedigree. The Brooklyn Nets forward has built a strong reputation around the NBA for his high skill level and dominance on the court. With all the good can come bad moments too. In 2017, a Los Angeles Times article came out entitled, "Kevin Durant Apparently Tried to Use a Fake Twitter Account to Defend Himself, slam Thunder."[12] The article states that "Durant appears to have been trying to use fake Twitter accounts to defend himself against haters on social media."[12] This article came out and showed evidence that Durant would reply to fans using what we call in the industry "burner account," an account someone anonymously operates so they can post without anything leading back to them.

The LA Times writer and other media outlets figured this out after KD forgot to turn off his burner account and instead replied to the haters from his personal account. He would reply tweet with insider news that only a player on the team would know. Tweets like "he didn't like the organization or playing for Billy Donovan," the Oklahoma City Thunder coach at the time.[12] Also, he talked in third person by replying to a tweet with "KD can't win a championship with those cats."[12] This became suspicious to fans as they wondered why he would be tweeting these things. Later on, these tweets were deleted, bringing more suspicion to the table.

I remember these articles about KD in 2017 while I was working at Bleacher Report. As someone who had been in sports social media for almost four years at the time, I thought, "What an idiot," wondering why he didn't just let the haters just criticize and troll like they always do. He's a multi-millionaire and one of the most famous NBA players of the 2010s but couldn't let the haters just be themselves. He had to defend himself, which is what you don't want to do in sports social media. Two-time World Series champion Hunter Pence said when dealing with trolls, "The greatest defense is no defense at all. Whenever you start defending yourself against something, then you've already lost. I try to just allow them to feel how they want and move in my own direction."[13]

Pence is right. Don't add gasoline to the fire. When you reply and defend yourself, you leave yourself open to more attacks from the trolls and haters. Not only that, but it can backfire and turn into bad publicity for the athlete. Pence added that KD will learn from this negative moment and grow from it. "There's lessons that make you a greater person even going through that situation. It was probably coming from love because he was hurt by those negative comments. He just wants love and there's nothing wrong with that," he said.[13]

It can take years of learning what to do and what not do in sports social media. I learned my lessons through errors I made in the past, so did Shanks and Tunsil, and I'm sure Durant did too. You live and learn from your experiences in your life. Negative and infamous moments may overshadow parts of your career, but eventually you'll see and understand that you can overcome any dilemma thrown your way. The positives will overshadow the negatives and you will come out stronger as a person.

> "Our bad memories and our bad experiences are
> what make us who we are and what make us grow
> and allow us to learn, if we choose to see the lessons
> in those experiences." —Elijah Wood[14]

CITATIONS:

1. Zyad Ismael, "Social Media's Affect On Sports: Pros And Cons," *The Flyer*, 2017, https://www.fairmontflyer.com/features/2017/04/04/26833/.

 accessed February 16, 2021, https://www.merriam-webster.com/dictionary/troll.

3. Brandon Curran, phone call with author, January 15, 2021.

4. Julie Phayer, phone call with the author, November 12, 2020.

5. Chad Shanks, phone call with author, February 9, 2021.

6. Chad Shanks Tweet, April 29, 2015. https://twitter.com/chadjshanks/status/593496214575788032

7. Nate Davis, "Mock Draft 2.0: First-Round Outlook After Super Bowl," USA TODAY, 2016, https://www.usatoday.com/story/sports/nfl/draft/2016/02/08/mock-draft-first-round-titans-browns/79973774/.

8., Kevin Seifert, "After Gas Mask Tweet, Tunsil Slides To Miami At 13," *ESPN* 2016, https://www.espn.com/nfl/draft2016/story/_/id/15423201/agent-laremy-tunsil-gas-mask-tweet-was-hacked.

9. Anthony Riccobono, "NFL Draft 2016 Contracts: Projected Salaries For All First-Round Picks,"International Business Times, 2016, https://www.ibtimes.com/nfl-draft-2016-contracts-projected-salaries-all-first-round-picks-2361279.

10. Andrew Abramson (@AbramsonFL) Tweet on April 30, 2016, https://twitter.com/AbramsonFL/status/726460038513045506

11. "Texans' Laremy Tunsil Signs 3-Year, $66M Extension," NFL, 2020. https://www.nfl.com/news/ texans-laremy-tunsil-signs-3-year-66m-extension-0ap3000001111084.

12. Chuck Schilken, 2017, "Kevin Durant Apparently Tried To Use A Fake Twitter Account To Defend Himself, Slam Thunder," *Los Angeles Times,* https://www.latimes.com/sports/sportsnow/la-sp-durant-twitter-fake-20170918-story.html.

13. Hunter Pence, phone call with the author, January 29, 2021.

14. "Elijah Wood Quote: 'Our Bad Memories And Our Bad Experiences Are What Make Us Who We Are And What Make Us Grow And Allow Us To Learn, If We …,'" *Quotefancy,* Accessed February 17, 2021, https:// quotefancy.com/quote/1474979/Elijah-Wood-Our-bad-memories-and-our-bad-experiences-are-what-make-us-who-we-are-and-what.

CHAPTER 12:
THE EVOLUTION OF ATHLETE SOCIAL MEDIA

"I think the biggest insight that I have about sports social media is that it's really driven first and foremost by the athletes because it gives them a chance to have a direct relationship with fans, in a way that they never could before," —Principal of Claygate Advisors David Sternberg[1]

Alot has changed, and athletes are leading the way in sports social media. Before, athletes were only able to share their voice and content through television, newspapers, and radio stations around the country. This was scary to players because they didn't have their own medium to express themselves and show the following what was going on with their life.

The concept of athletes having their own voice didn't happen before social media took over in the early 2010s. The media was the only way for athletes to get their opinions out to the world, and they were subject to whatever a journalist would write or say about them. "Before we had our own voice, the only thing that people got their news from was the newspaper or what journalists said. Let's say we had a fifteen-minute interview. They could cut one little piece of this whole long thing out of context," two-time World Series champion Hunter Pence said.[2] Pence said that the public felt disconnected from the athlete because all they knew about the athlete "is through the writer who you're very connected to because you've read them for years and years and years, and they can kind of paint whatever story they want."[2]

One of Pence's favorite platforms to use is Twitter. He launched his Twitter account in mid-2010s during his fourth season in the majors. When I asked about what his teammates, coaches, and the front office thought about his social media usage, his answer intrigued me. "They did not like it for many years. It was very looked down upon. You were definitely bashed for having a Twitter or whatever social media account," he said.[2] It's very interesting because although Twitter and other platforms gave the athletes the opportunity to use their voice, certain players were against it. I believe players didn't want other players to talk about what was happening the locker room (still kept secret to this day) to their social media audience. Eventually, the tide turned for the athletes that were hating on Pence's social media usage. They would say to Pence, "'Hey I started Twitter account, can you tweet it out?' and it's a weird cycle and obviously I'm like, 'Whatever, any way I can help.'"[2]

Not only did players' attitudes toward social media change over time but also other parts of the organization changed. "It is starting to change in the clubhouse where it's like, 'Hey, you got to do this as part of being a baseball player as part of, your brand, your life.' Teams are now having meetings about some of the best ways to use social media because it is also attached to the team that you're on because you are a representation of the team," Pence said.[2]

The evolution of MLB social media is very interesting to me because of how it changed drastically in a short period of time. Obviously, teams want to educate their players because they don't want their athletes to make a mistake on social media and potentially affect the entire organization. The acceptance and love of social media spread like that wildfire in that season two episode of Game of Thrones. I hope I didn't spoil the episode, but it's been about two years since the show ended.

I'm glad social media has given athletes a voice because it allows them to have a stronger connection with the fans. "Technology and increased media exposure have given professional athletes a greater platform to have their opinions heard on any aspect of society and not just restricted to sports. Social media has also allowed these athletes to present themselves to their fans as they see themselves, in a more personable way."[3] Athletes are now allowed to be themselves more than ever. They don't have to worry about being judged or their quotes being misconstrued by the media. From the fan perspective, there's more of a connection with their favorite players, which can only increase their connection to an athlete.

"You get to tell the story through your eyes. You get to connect with the fans how you want to. Social media has given the players so much more strength to just have authenticity and to have their own voice. So it changed all of media in and of itself," Pence said.[2] There was a moment in the mid-2010s where Pandora's box opened and flipped the media/social media world on its head. The evolution didn't stop there. Athletes now have the opportunity to be content creators and ideation experts and drive revenue from the platforms. Although each professional league has their own viewpoint on the how their athletes should use social media, all of them know it's important for every athlete's brand to have it. Social media is so much more than a platform for content, for it has allowed athletes to have the voice that they didn't have before.

THE RISE OF VLOGGERS IN THE NBA BUBBLE

Not only has social media amplified the athlete's voice, but athletes turning into content creators is on the rise as well. From the rise of "Taco Tuesday" and family dance videos with LeBron James to numerous other athletes taking social media into their own hands. James has also created Uninterrupted, a media company dedicated to empowering athletes and inspiring people. Seahawks QB Russell Wilson has his own brand management and production company called WEST2EAST EMPIRE. KD created Thirty-Five Ventures in order to do a variety of things, including a media department dedicated to developing content (both long form and short form). This is just a small list of what athletes are doing with their money and star power to create brands in the sports content world. It's very impressive to see the rise of content-first companies that make an impact in our society.

One example that stands out to me is the vlogging that former Lakers Center JaVale McGee and 76ers guard Matisse Thybulle did during the NBA bubble in Orlando, Florida. "Vlogs, or blogs that contain video material, became a forefront of players' social media experiences."[4] During the 2020 season, to maintain a safe and healthy environment during the COVID-19 pandemic, the NBA hosted numerous games, including the NBA Finals at the ESPN Wide World of Sports Complex. The players were tested multiple times per day and weren't allowed to leave the facility. This lasted from July–October 2020. This was very successful as the NBA had no reported cases for all of the teams participating in the bubble. "We had zero positive tests for as long as we were here, 90-some days, 95 days maybe for myself. I had a little calendar I was checking off. But on a serious note, no positive tests. That's a success for everybody that was involved," James said in a Los Angeles Times article.[5]

That wasn't the only successful note from the NBA bubble. NBA players McGee, Thybulle, and Troy Daniels all vlogged from Orlando to show an inside look of what the players were going through. All three players built a strong YouTube following from their vlogging episodes.

The biggest growth came from McGee who increased his following in the hundreds of thousands. McGee launched his YouTube channel right after the 2018 NBA Finals. His first video was of him vlogging at the Golden State Warriors championship parade. McGee was garnering views in the several thousands for a while, but his account took off during the NBA bubble, so much so that he went on to hire a video producer, Devin Dismang, to help manage the content creation. McGee would vlog from Orlando, and Dismang would edit and upload the videos to YouTube.

The idea started as a casual idea that turned into something creative and unique. McGee said to Dismang, "Hey, I got my camera, do you think I should bring it?" Dismang said back to McGee, "Why not, you could probably film things over there and we can figure it out."[6] Dismang said that it wasn't this profound idea. Dismang told McGee to film himself getting on the plane headed to Orlando and that he would upload it to the YouTube page to see how it performed. They did two more videos, and the videos were doing "decent."[6] Finally, Dismang uploaded the third video with the title "team scrimmage" and closed his computer for the night.

The next day, McGee and Dismang saw all three videos each hit over one million views. Dismang said that fans found the videos on YouTube, and it started taking off as more and more people watched them. The fans loved getting inside footage from the exclusive NBA bubble. "You see Danny Green on the bus, you're seeing a clip of LeBron on a plane, and you see Anthony Davis saying, 'What's up?' on the camera," Dismang said.[6] Fans loved getting inside footage of top NBA players during the bubble, and the videos quickly took off as they displayed the star power on the Lakers. "We have a camera inside the Orlando bubble from a starting Los Angeles Laker, who plays with LeBron James and Anthony Davis, during the craziest time in NBA history. We're going to lock it on that," Dismang said.[6]

Dismang said that McGee's subscribers went from thirty-five thousand to one hundred thousand in under a week. This series was episodic content that ranged from eight to seventeen minutes per video. In under six weeks, McGee's account hit the half a million-subscriber milestone. Each "Life in the Bubble" video got between 800,000 to 2.4 million views. McGee ended up doing nineteen "Life in the Bubble" episodes, which totaled over 23 million views or around 1.2 million views per video.

McGee and Dismang took advantage of a very slow content time in the NBA and were successful because they were getting content from "the world's most exclusive place and not that much media could get in," Dismang said.[6] Also the content was perfect for what the audience was looking for, an inside look into the NBA bubble and the Lakers, who then went on to win their seventeenth championship. Now McGee has nearly seven hundred thousand subscribers and a very loyal fanbase thanks to his content from the NBA bubble.

McGee wasn't the only player vlogging from the NBA bubble. Thybulle ended up getting content from Orlando too. He was actually a bit of a rival to McGee in terms of athlete content creators there. In July 2020, Thybulle started his YouTube channel with zero subscribers. He decided to create the series "Welcome to the Bubble," which followed him and his teammates' journey in Florida. As he said, "I've always wanted to create videos. My friends and I have messed around developing content for a long time, but with the NBA entering the bubble, I had a good reason to create."[7] So Thybulle created content all by himself, doing videography and editing. "I had nothing to lose and my 'Welcome to the Bubble' vlogs were a good test. The NBA bubble had never happened before in the history, and people wanted to have an inside look," Thybulle said.[7] Thybulle's first video recorded 1.5 million views and 63,000 likes! Thybulle would end up uploading nine "Welcome to the Bubble" episodes during his time in Orlando. Videos ranged from 400,000 to 1.5 million views per episode. Thybulle garnered over eight million views or almost one million views per episode.

Similar to McGee's page, Thybulle's page saw tremendous growth in short period of time. In less than two months, Thybulle racked up over three hundred thousand subscribers! When asked about the fast growth of the page, Thybulle responded by saying, "No, I never imagined or expected the vlogs to be such a big hit. I was able to create content that I love, and YouTube was the right platform to share with the masses."[7] Fans loved Thybulle's vlogging style and how he was filming the NBA bubble almost like a documentarian. Thybulle doesn't have any immediate plans to grow his social media following, but he clearly struck gold during a short period of time.

McGee and Thybulle took advantage of the circumstance they were both in. In an NBA bubble where content was like a drought in the middle of the sandy desert, these two athletes vlogged as if they were the mirage to the fans. But this mirage was actually real. They were content creators in one of the most exclusive places in the world. Both have built a strong subscriber base, and while they aren't star players like LeBron or Durant, they have carved out a niche: basketball players who can ball on the court but also create amazing content off the court.

TISHA ALYN—FROM ATHLETE TO INFLUENCER

Not everyone's route is like McGee's and Thybulle's because not all athletes have an enthusiasm for social media. Some athletes have been able to capitalize over the last few years as the word 'content creator' can also be synonymous to 'influencer.' "Influencers in social media are people who have built a reputation for their knowledge and expertise on a specific topic. They make regular posts about that topic on their preferred social media channels and generate large followings of enthusiastic, engaged people who pay close attention to their views."[8] Athletes can not only be influencers while they are playing professionally, but when their career ends, they can turn into an influencer and have a second career. That happened with Tisha Alyn Abrea, a former professional golfer turned media personality and influencer. PGA. com wrote a story about Abrea entitled "Inspiring the Future of the Game."[9]

Abrea has carved out a niche as a former professional golfer who is amazing at creating unique content that really resonates with her followers. Even though I am a golf fan and was an average high school golfer, I not only like Tisha as a golf content creator but also for how she shows different sides of herself. From her amazing dance moves to trick shots to a skit to showcasing a brand in a golf video. She has a lot of content buckets she can hit from and is always unapologetically herself. "Authenticity is it. If you want to be in social media, that is literally the word you must have in your vocabulary. The overarching message is that you have to be authentic because that's what influencers do. Influencers are named their name because we truly influence the following that you have," Abrea said.[10] The power of the influencer is to influence the audience. It's as simple as that. The content you create should have an impact on your following, and you'll grow new followers if the content resonates.

I'm not sure if "influencer" is the title that Abrea wants to give herself. Her Instagram bio reads "Golf Media Personality, Content Creator, Pro Golf, Dancer, Trickster and Certified Instructor." I believe she wants to be more than just an influencer as that title could be very trendy these days. Her Instagram account has over two hundred followers, but what has really taken off is her TikTok channel. She has nearly six hundred thousand followers and has had over six million likes combined through her videos. One of her most famous TikTok videos was where she hit a ball deep with her driver at night on a driving range. Seems like a regular video, but it received 14.6 million views and 250,000 likes! It was one of the most viral golf TikTok videos of all-time, maybe even the most.

What's next for Abrea? "I think I am pretty close to being known as one of the top creators in the golf space. I hope to maintain that title for as long as I decide to do this. I know social media will be around for a while, but I hope to keep up that creativity," she said.[10] Abrea's dreams and aspirations doesn't stop at social media. She hopes to potentially have a TV spot one day as well. She's an inspiration because she turned her professional golf career into a thriving media personality and influencer career. She's a great example for any athlete that wants to do the same after their career is over.

Doesn't matter if you're a professional athlete in the MLB, NBA, golf, or any other sport. You have the opportunity to show your voice, became a content creator, and influence your audience. The perception of social media has changed in the sports world from Pence's early days with Twitter in 2010/2011 where teammates looked down upon him to now where professional leagues and teams encourage social media on their players. Athletes are not only using social media to use their voice and post content relevant to their lives but also as a revenue generator. Abrea finished our conversation by adding how much these brands mean to her life. "These partnerships are everything to me, and I think from an outside perspective, maybe to the average follower they may just think like, 'I'm following her because she's entertaining,' but like to me, this is my livelihood, and I'm very fortunate to do what I love for a living," she said.[10]

CITATIONS:

1. David Sternberg, phone call with the author, November 17, 2020.

2. Hunter Pence, phone call with the author, January 29, 2021.

3. Charles Freeman, "The Social Evolution Of Athletes," *The Sport Digest,* 2018, http://thesportdigest.com/2018/10/the-social-evolution-of-athletes/.

4. Merriam-Webster, s.v. "vlog (n.)," accessed February 14, 2021, https://www.merriam-webster.com/dictionary/vlog.

5. Kelcie Pegher, "Coronavirus Today: The NBA's Bubble Worked," Los Angeles Times, 2020, https://www.latimes.com/science/newsletter/2020-10-12/coronavirus-today-nba-bubble-success-covid-lakers-coronavirus-today.

6. Devin Dismang, phone call with the author, December 8, 2020.

7. Matisse Thybulle, email with the author, January 12, 2021.

8. "What Is An Influencer? - Social Media Influencers Defined [Updated 2021]," *Influencer Marketing Hub,* 2021, https://influencermarketinghub.com/what-is-an-influencer/.

9. Carly Grenfell, "Tisha Alyn Abrea: Inspiring the Future of the Game," PGA, 2020, https://www.pga.com/story/fairway-tales-tisha-alyn-abrea-inspiring-the-future-of-the-game.

10. Tisha Abrea, phone call with the author, February 12, 2021.

CHAPTER 13:

THE GROWTH OF ATHLETE MONETIZATION ON SOCIAL MEDIA

"Everybody wants to get paid. Everybody loves
money, whether you say you do or don't,"
—NBA player Troy Daniels[1]

Money makes the world go around. In capitalist America, money is what drives most people. You need to make money to survive in this world. It's the stark but real truth in our society. This is no different for athletes in the sports world. They need to earn money to support their families, to not go bankrupt, and to have a future where they don't struggle. The common misconception with athletes is that they're all millionaires and live successful lives. This is not true for most athletes because unless you're in one of the top four sports in the US (NFL, NBA, MLB, and NHL), you could have a tough time capitalizing off the contract money.

With a strong agency and marketing team around you as an athlete, you could be successful, but not all have that luxury. Many athletes in the minor leagues need to find alternative sources of income to balance their contract money. "I kind of realized that being a minor leaguer is not very sustainable. The goal is to get to the major leagues, and you obviously can make a good living doing that. I think right away when I got drafted, I realized that for me to keep playing baseball, keep chasing my dream I had to do something else," professional baseball player Alex Katz said.[2] Katz is one of many players who uses their brand off the field to generate revenue. The average minor-league baseball player can earn between $6,050-$14,850 per year for playing between Low-A to AAA league.[3] The federally recognized poverty line is at $12,140 per year for single-individual households.[3] It was shocking to me when I found this out. No wonder Katz and other minor leaguers need to find alternative sources of income. The pitcher has an Instagram following of over fifty thousand people where he makes money off brands like Jabra headphones, Knockaround sunglasses, and other companies.

Not only is Katz generating revenue from social media, but he is also an entrepreneur. He is a partner in CleatClear and Frost Gear and is extremely proud of Stadium Custom Kicks, which has double the following of its founder at over 117,000. Stadium Custom Kicks is "a custom footwear company that creates custom shoes and cleats. Not just for professional athletes but for kids and pretty much any person," he said.[2] It's a successful business that Katz was very excited to talk about. "We work with over one thousand professional athletes, so that's obviously our biggest market right now," he said.[2]

Katz has figured out what he needs to do to be successful off the field. Baseball can only pay so much, especially if you don't turn into a longtime player in the majors. Katz is proud of the money he generates off his social media accounts and believes more brands need to continue to pay athletes to do the same. There is value an athlete brings to the table that would be helpful for brands to associate themselves with. "I think you'd get a lot more for your money by paying an athlete to post on their social media page, especially if they have a loyal following," Katz said.[2] Athletes are turning into influencers themselves because they want a piece of the pie. They have a tremendous platform that a brand can champion, especially if that athlete has success on the field, court, or wherever they play. The main decision is which companies are going to go with which athletes, based on what makes the most sense with their brand values. It's a bit of a matchmaking process when it comes to athletes getting the right brand for their social media channels and the same goes for the brand.

THE IMPACT OF JUJU SMITH-SCHUSTER'S SOCIAL MEDIA

Certain athletes are taking advantage of social media and making a name for themselves off the field. They get brands to sponsor them off the field because they have a large and loyal following. One player that's transcended the sports world in terms of social media is Steelers WR JuJu Smith-Schuster aka JuJu. He has turned into the gold standard of the young athlete on social media these days and what enormous revenue they can generate. JuJu has literally turned into a brand, and it all started during his rookie season in the NFL when he launched his YouTube channel.

His YouTube videos have given fans an inside look into his life and shown off his unique and engaging personality. The YouTube community bought in right around the inception of his account and have stayed loyal ever since. JuJu has made videos about pranking Steelers fans by doing undercover interviews, buying swag for all fans that were shopping in an Adidas store, and going to a fan's prom, which have all garnered over one million views on YouTube. Twelve of his videos have reached over one million views. But the most successful video that really launched him as a social media star was when he pranked USC students and teachers by going back to his alma mater in full Steelers gear. In February 2018, the seventeen-minute video received nearly 10 million views and 179,000 likes. The video went viral on YouTube and really showed other athletes to step up their social media game if they wanted to compete with the young WR. JuJu invested into his social media career right when his playing days were just beginning.

Without even mentioning his name, when I asked numerous social media experts what athletes were standing out in social media, many brought up JuJu and the impact he is having. "His personality lends itself to social media. When he was drafted, instead of bragging about getting a fancy car, he was posting videos of him sweeping the alley behind his mom's house, and it was very authentic and raw. This is a guy who just made himself millions and millions of dollars, but he's still showing you the less glamorous sides of his life. That made him really relatable, authentic, and made him a must-follow," Rael Enteen said.[4] JuJu has had the perfect strategy for each social media platform, and it shows. Juju knows how to put long-form videos on YouTube, dance videos/short form on TikTok, and tailormade content on Instagram. He executes well, and whether you're a Steelers fan or not, you can become a JuJu fan because of not just his play on the field, but his game-changing social media accounts.

"He has been the blueprint of what a current athlete or young player should be doing in the field, and has branded himself in such a unique way," President of Maxx MGMT Maxx Lepselter said.[5]

Across Facebook, Instagram, Twitter, YouTube, and TikTok, JuJu now has over ten million followers. Not the same numbers as LeBron James, but I believe he makes a significant impact on the younger generation of NFL fans. I remember during my time at Bleacher Report, JuJu wasn't too far behind LeBron and Warriors guard Stephen Curry in terms of the number of times we reposted his videos. His videos are engaging and funny and connect well to the Gen Z and millennial fanbase. This has led to brands all wanting a piece of JuJu and his loyal following. JuJu has partnerships with Adidas, Oakley, HyperX (a headphone company), and Pizza Hut to name a few.

At the 2018 NFL draft (the year after JuJu was drafted), he showed up wearing a Pizza Hut suit with a custom blazer and bow tie. Pizza Hut wanted to show off their new deal as the official pizza of the NFL, and JuJu made a splash at the draft that he wasn't even getting drafted in. If you look over his Instagram page, you can see posts he's done to show partnerships with Oikos, Art of Sport, Xbox, Hyperice, and DAZN. He has turned into one of the most marketable players in the NFL and maybe all of sports because of his loyal social media following. Just like Lepselter said, I'm sure other athletes in the NFL and other professional leagues will look to replicate JuJu's blueprint, so that they can also generate marketing revenue. But I'm not sure they will be as successful since his brand is authentic and highly engaging.

VOLLEYBALL'S MCKIBBIN BROTHERS APPROACH TO BRANDED CONTENT

Not everyone can make the marketing dollars like a professional athlete from one of the top four sports in the US. JuJu is unique case of how an NFL player can build a social media empire from nothing. It's not easy for other athletes, especially the Olympic sports. In case you didn't know, "most Olympians don't receive any compensation for simply competing in the Olympics. Despite not having a national average salary, Olympians can earn funding from a variety of sources including corporate sponsorships, endorsement deals, and medal bonuses."[6]

Endorsement deals and partnerships have become a necessity to survive and pay Olympians' monthly expenses. In the past, the top 1% of Olympic athletes actually make money from endorsement deals, but times are changing with the growth of athlete monetization. Athletes can get paid to post a piece of branded or sponsored content on their accounts. Two athletes who are doing some creative things on social media and seeing brands pay for their accounts as ad space are the McKibbin brothers (Riley and Maddison). The McKibbin brothers are professional beach volleyball players and YouTube content creators. The brothers are both Association of Volleyball Professionals (AVP) members and play at the highest level of beach volleyball.

They have built one of the top YouTube channels in their sport with over ninety thousand followers. They have a loyal following of not just volleyball enthusiasts but other sports fans too. They are well known for their knowledge of the sport, their charisma, and their iconic beards that might be on par with NBA superstar James Harden's beard. They have had numerous videos go over 250,000 views on YouTube. Riley said that he wasn't too keen on using social media growing up but eventually saw it as a resource for his professional volleyball career. "We started viewing it as a tool, especially when we transferred from indoor volleyball to beach volleyball," he said.[7] While in indoor volleyball, you are under contract and paid a salary, but in beach volleyball, you are playing for winnings. It's just how the two leagues separate their pay systems for their athletes. Mainly the reason that social media became important to them is because "a lot of your income is derived from sponsorships," he said.[7]

The brothers decided to go the YouTube route over Instagram because they wanted to show brands and potential partnerships the value of the platform. Also, YouTube was lacking beach volleyball content at the time. "There was almost like zero coverage except for games from the 90s," Riley said.[7] Video production is something the brothers have been interested in for a long time, so YouTube was the perfect medium to show their YouTube knowledge and grow their content creation skills. YouTube has turned into a major part of their lives because it provides revenue for the brothers outside of beach volleyball winnings. "That's essentially our full-time job now. Playing can be a career, but you have to be one of the top four teams to really make a decent living out of it," Riley said.[7] The brothers have turned to branded content to add another income stream. The have partnered with Wilson Volleyball, Lululemon Athletica, and Sharpe Vision, a Lasik eye company.

One of their longtime partners has been Wilson Volleyball. The brothers were hired to make a YouTube video for AVP Media Day. Maddison said that the normal questions they got were "stupid," but they wanted to create a branded content video to get an inside look into "who these players were."[8] So that's what the brothers did. "We were able to get the true essence or just a pure response from these athletes," Maddison said.[8] In the 2020 AVP Media Day, the fifteen-minute video garnered over twenty-five thousand views and eight hundred likes. Might not seem like a lot compared to some of their other YouTube videos, but this was long-form branded content in action. Most branded content doesn't perform as well as original content, but their video performed well, something the brothers can hang their hat on and be proud of. I watched the full video, and it was super engaging because they titled the video "The Black Book of the AVP," and players in the video spilled the beans on other players.

What's next for the brothers in terms of their social media channels and monetization? Continue to make more money away from the beach. "It's been really great working with a lot of these brands. I guess the perfect recipe for success on social is working with a brand like Wilson. Wilson Sporting Goods has given us free rein to do what we want and what we know works is great storytelling. It needs to be at the core of everything we create," Riley said.[7] Even if you're not a fan of volleyball, the McKibbin brothers do a great job of not only storytelling but also education on the sport. They want to continue to work with companies that want to do branded content and build long-term partnerships. If they can continue to do that, the sky is the limit for the brothers on social media.

ATHLETE MONETIZATION TOOLS HELP ATHLETES GENERATE REVENUE

Not only can athletes reach out to brands and vice versa but also there are tools to streamline the process of athlete monetization. Athletes like the McKibbin brothers can really benefit from companies like Opendorse and OpenSponsorship.

Both are tools that allow any athlete from the NBA to gymnastics to make money from social media. They connect brands with athletes to generate more revenue for the athlete. Although they are competitors, they both make the athlete monetization world a lot better. Social media monetization was irrelevant for athletes eight-plus years ago, but now it is one of the most thriving markets for an athlete's revenue off the field and court.

Opendorse was started by two University of Nebraska football players after they graduated from school. "Why we started Opendorse is really to do the same thing that I did which is use social media to build an audience that will last well after their playing days are done," Opendorse CEO Blake Lawrence said.[9] The company is now helping more than fifty thousand athletes around the world with monetization. One of Lawrence's past Nebraska teammates, Prince Amukamara, asked Lawrence three questions after he made it to the NFL in 2011, which have become important for Opendorse clients to this day.

1) What is the value of my audience?
2) How do I grow my audience?
3) How do I monetize my audience?

Amukamara's sports agency wasn't helping him answer those questions, and there wasn't a sophisticated technology tool that agencies used at the time. So Lawrence and his business partner Adi Kunalic decided to take matters into their own hands and make the first tool to help athletes answer these questions. "Let's build a solution for Prince, so he can understand his audience, get content to grow it, and monetize it with one tap. If it works for him, then maybe it'll work for others," Lawrence said.[9] By March 2013, Lawrence and Kunalic were flying out to Washington DC to meet with the NFL Players Association. Once there, they talked about a partnership to help every NFL player, and that is where Opendorse took off. Opendorse needed to build trust with these athletes and the way to do that was to bring value within the first sixty to ninety days. The value was paid opportunities to work with brands in the partnerships space.

In 2015, athletes started to notice how teammates in the locker room were getting more deals because they were marketable via their social media accounts. "This whole movement for athletes who need to start looking at social media as a mechanism for earning those brand deals, but most athletes aren't natural marketers," Lawrence said.[9] Opendorse helps with that problem. Opendorse can post on thirty thousand athletes' social media accounts because of their access. It's there to help athletes not screw up a deal by using the wrong hashtags, tagging the wrong accounts, or any other potential mistakes. Opendorse will only continue to develop their platform as five hundred thousand student athletes can now monetize their brands because Name, Image, and Likeness rules have opened up. "Most simply, 'name, image and likeness' are three elements that make up a legal concept known as 'right of publicity.' Right of publicity involves those situations where permission is required of a person to use their name, image or likeness."[10]

OpenSponsorship is another athlete monetization tool that has created a platform for over eight thousand athletes. Some of the athletes that are on OpenSponsorship include nontraditional sports like lacrosse. "We have athletes in lacrosse who tell us if it wasn't for OpenSponsorship, they wouldn't be able to play full-time in the league. It could be a way to just supplement their income for the bigger guys too," CEO and founder of OpenSponsorship Ishveen Anand said.[11] The future plan for OpenSponsorship is how to help those half-million student athletes navigate the athlete monetization market. Dealing with the brands is the first step to success. "We will be the best place for brands to come and do these deals. We want to make sure that their money is well-spent. We believe that if we keep focusing on the brand side, then you know the end of the day the athlete is going to go with where brands are, and hopefully that will be us," Anand said.[11]

Either way, with the market shifting for athlete monetization in the student-athlete space, it will be exciting to see how deals get done with brands and which athletes will come out on top. Athletes will continue to look for alternative sources of income because the contract money can only last for so long. Whether you're a baseball, football, or volleyball player, you are always looking to find means to add another revenue stream or bolster a current one that you have. Athletes are and will continue to turn into influencers in our society because of the impact they make on the sports world, and monetization will continue to come their way. Continue to keep an eye out for which of your favorite athletes are doing which deals that make sense for them because it's only going to increase in the coming years.

Actor Cuba Gooding Jr. played an athlete (Rod Tidwell) in the movie Jerry Maguire, and his famous line couldn't be truer now and in the future for athlete monetization: "Show me the money!"

CITATIONS:

1. Troy Daniels, phone call with the author, January 22, 2021.

2. Alex Katz, phone call with the author, December 17, 2020.

3. Levi Weaver, "On Minor-League Pay, MLB's Stance Doesn't Line Up With The Facts," *The Athletic,* 2018, https://theathletic.com/293189/2018/04/04/ on-minor-league-pay-mlbs-stance-doesnt-line-up-with-the-facts/.

4. Rael Enteen, phone call with the author, December 3, 2020.

5. Maxx Lepselter, phone call with the author, December 16, 2020.

6. "How Much Do Olympians Make?" 2021, *Indeed,* https://www.in-deed.com/career-advice/pay-salary/how-much-do-olympians-make.

7. Riley McKibbin, phone call with the author, January 15, 2021.

8. Maddison McKibbin, phone call with the author, December 3, 2020.

9. Blake Lawrence, phone call with the author, January 12, 2021.

10. Rachel Stark-Mason, "Name, Image, Likeness" *NCAA*, Accessed February 18, 2021, https://www.ncaa.org/champion/name-image-likeness.

11. Ishveen Anand, phone call with the author, December 17, 2020.

CHAPTER 14:

LESSONS LEARNED FROM THE PAST WILL CONTINUE IN THE FUTURE

"I don't know what the future may hold, but I know who holds the future." —Ralph Abernathy[1]

How does Abernathy, a civil rights activist, connect to sports social media? The future of sports social media is unknown. There is constant change from the consumption habits of the audience to the development of new platforms. One year, Facebook is the sexy shiny new toy, and it beats out MySpace in terms of popularity. Now, Facebook is used by the younger generation's parents and grandparents, and therefore it's not cool anymore. The millennials might be spending more time on Instagram and the Gen Zers might be on TikTok, but that could all change, and part of this book could be irrelevant next year. The future of sports social media is unknown, but the future of the industry is largely driven by younger generations who are deeply connected to the ever-changing technology.

I can't predict what platforms the younger generations will use in 2022 let alone 2025, but what I do know is that change will come because the consumption habits of the younger generations will change. They might have loved Facebook one day, but it's Instagram the next, then it's TikTok, and so forth. I'm not here to be Nostradamus or wave my hands in front of a crystal ball. What I do know is that there will be some consistent themes with the future of sports social media that you need to be aware of. There are three main themes that will remain true in the coming years.

First, original content will always be the true differentiator among competition. In my mind, content will always be king, especially in sports social media. If you want to stand out among the crowd, your content needs to be the way to do it. Your content needs to be unique, funny, and engaging, some of the qualities I look for when a sports social media account posts original content. Although in high school, there were groups like the jocks, nerds, goths, and more, it's best to create your own lane and be unique, and the same goes for original content. Some sports companies will always be better than others in terms of original content because they have hired the right ideators and creators to be the difference among competition. When you have the right people in place, you can have success on social media, and the fans will show you love through loyalty to your brand and engagement on your posts.

Next, athlete-first content will continue to grow over time. Athletes like LeBron James, Stephen Curry, and Russell Wilson have already taken advantage of using their star power to develop a brand on social media. Other athletes will follow, and some are already doing so. JaVale McGee has a specific strategy that fits his audience, and he has picked up new followers because his original content is engaging. When I asked NBA player Troy Daniels which players he sees a good example from on social media, his answer was simple. "McGee is the number one guy. He creates content and still plays basketball at a high level. He is taking advantage of his social media, and the audience notices," he said.[2] If more players continue to follow the lead of McGee and other social media savvy players, then there will eventually be a saturation of athlete content. More players will start to hire content teams, or their agencies will provide content creators, so that they will not only succeed on social media but thrive. This is one trend that most of the people I talked to expected would continue to grow in the future.

Finally, sports social media revenue will increase as it has over the last six years. Brands will continue to pour more money into companies and athletes' social media for the purpose of continuing to increase brand equity. We will see the influx of new deals left and right. More companies will be putting their marketing dollars toward social media because that's where the younger generations are. Followers of companies, teams, and athletes on social media can expect to see more branded social media posts, which might not be the best thing. The audience knows what branded and sponsored content looks like and will continue to see right through it as it permeates their news feed.

So brands will need to become creative with what sponsored content they put on the audience's news feed. It can't be an overt sponsored post anymore; it needs to be a well-integrated branded content post that shows off the partner without being in the audience's face with logos and such. I believe with the increase of branded content will come changes to the algorithm that might help or hurt those posts depending on the platform. Either way, the audience should be prepared for more branded and sponsored content because social media accounts need to generate revenue, and that's the best way to do it.

ORIGINAL CONTENT WILL ALWAYS BE RELEVANT

Original content is what can make or break a sports social media account. It allows accounts to stand out among the saturation of the news feed. Various sports accounts will need to think two steps ahead of the competition when it comes to original content. The production of original content will only increase per account in the future. During Hankins' time with the LA Kings in the early 2010s, they were not only competing with other NHL accounts, but also sports accounts in their own city. From the Lakers to the Clippers to the Dodgers, Hankins said that "in order for us to stand out we needed to be engaging."[3] Being engaging is what all major sports social media accounts need to think about because you need your followers to interact with the content so that they can remember it.

Former social media director at the UFC Randy Faehnrich explained how working in social media means you have to have the creative chops. "We are content creators at our core. I think a lot of people don't realize how creative people in the social space are. How creative they have to be in order to create original content," he said.[4] Not everyone has that creativity to succeed in sports social media, and that's okay. If you want to have success in the sports social media industry, then original content is the way to go.

Bill Gates said in 1996 that "Content is King," and the essay/statement remains true to this day. Every sports social media account needs people on the team that think of what content will be successful and engaging to the audience. It's imperative to be forward-thinking in this field because there will be more content saturation in the future, and you need stand out among the crowd. If you don't, like I've said before, you stand a chance of falling behind the competition. As a sports social media account, that's the last thing you want to do. The players in the game of sports social media will change over time, but one thing that will remain constant is original content will always be relevant.

MORE ATHLETES WILL DOUBLE-DOWN ON CONTENT CREATION

We've already seen the trend headed in the right direction with athletes being in control and having creative say over their content. This will only increase tenfold in the future. Other athletes have noticed which of their teammates are on social media and which are successful with it. Not everyone can be a LeBron, Curry, or Wilson, but some will come out of the fold and find ways to increase their content production and gain new followers. In this case, if you increase the supply of posts, you increase the demand from your following. Opendorse CEO Blake Lawrence agreed with this sentiment. Lawrence said that the average North American pro athlete will share six pieces of content per month. Compared to the average sports team, who will share sixty pieces of content per day, and average influencer, who will share six pieces of content per day. "Athletes are so far behind in terms of their content distribution. If they increase their content distribution, their engagement rate stays the same. It's one of the only instances in all of social media that the more you share, the more your fans engage," he said.[5]

The increase of posts is important to every athlete in the future. Blake Lawrence explained that original content is what will help athletes stand out from the rest. He also said there's a simple approach that more athletes should be adhering to in the future. "If every athlete shared a photo before a game and after a game, they would grow their audience at a much more rapid pace," he said.[5] "The more the merrier" rings true in athlete social media. McGee and Thybulle were just the tip of the iceberg in terms of what athletes could be doing on social media. Both increased their subscribers on YouTube by nearly four hundred thousand each during their time in the NBA bubble. It was just two NBA players giving an inside look into a heavily protected area in Orlando.

Both had great filming from a vlogging perspective, and the editing was exceptional. But their success can be replicated. More athletes can get into vlogging on YouTube, dancing on TikTok, or high-end highlight videos on Instagram as some examples. Athletes and their management teams can figure out which clients like which platforms and develop a strategy based around that. Not every platform has the same strategy, which means what you put on Instagram might not work for YouTube, and that's okay. But what athletes need to realize is they can attack each platform like a general with a battle strategy.

You just need to hire someone like myself, Toledano, Omar, the Malamut brothers, or any other ideator and creator to make you shine on social media. Finding the right people can take some time, but it will pay off in the long run. I say this because more people from the younger generations will want to get into social media, and if you find the right ones, you can build a social media team or eventually a media company around them, like LeBron, Curry, Wilson, and KD have.

I firmly believe that people are the greatest resource to any sports social media account. If you have the right people in place, then you can succeed on social media and potentially extend your career a few more years after your playing days are over. "The last conclusive research done on it showed that the average NBA player played for roughly 4.8 years."[6] "The average NFL career for all positions is only about two-and-a-half years."[7] I say this because you have to make the most of your playing career while it's happening. You need to capitalize on marketing during your playing career, so that you can extend yourself after you retire. Younger athletes are growing up on social media, which gets them to build their accounts at a young age. While they're playing professional sports, they will look to increase their content output to increase their followers. If you have don't take advantage of the fame, other athletes will surpass you in publicity.

Founder and CEO of Visionary Sports Karan Gill who helps manage JuJu Smith-Schuster discussed how athletes need to take advantage of social media at an early stage of their careers. "The biggest problem with athletes today is they don't necessarily care about social media that much, and marketing professionals and agencies don't put in the time to strategize and guide these athletes on how to navigate it early," he said.[8] Athletes need to start caring more and more because social media impacts their whole career, not just on the court and on the field but off it too. If more athletes create social media content teams around them, then they will reap the benefits not only during their career but after they retire because a strong social media following leads to more marketing, TV, and appearances, not to mention more revenue on social media which will only increase in the future.

REVENUE WILL INCREASE YEAR AFTER YEAR

With original content and athlete content increasing in the future, so will revenue. The money train isn't stopping anytime soon in the sports social media world; it's only picking up steam. Social media sales will increase through influencer marketing via athletes in the coming years. According to Industry Today, "Sports-related businesses, as well as those involved in health and fitness products and services, know that they can increase revenue by reaching out to a suitable athlete with an excellent social media fan base."[9] Athletes will continue to profit from social media if they have the loyal following that most brands are looking for these days. Not only will athletes profit, but also media companies like ESPN and Bleacher Report will earn tons of revenue from social media.

Teams will generate revenue from social media, which has become more important than ever with the COVID-19 pandemic destroying ticket sales (for good reason, of course). President and CEO of the Portland Trail Blazers Chris McGowan has seen how the pandemic has affected his team. "While they can't come to your arena, only 1% of your fan base actually comes to a game. The way you connect with those 99% of fans that aren't coming to games is the way you're going to grow as an organization," he said.[10]

COVID-19 really affected the way teams will produce income. Teams will have to continue to use social media as a revenue generator because they are losing money from ticket sales, merchandise, and food and drinks as well as other in-arena revenue. The team can succeed by generating more money from digital activity as a whole. I'm suspecting more teams will build out social sales departments to generate the money they are losing from other parts of the business.

Athletes need to look out for their best interests when it comes to marketing. Pence has partnered with companies like Fabletics, Nike, and Hulu to generate more revenue even after his playing days are over. There's always a personal reason behind which brands Pence will partner with. "All of the companies that I get to work with is usually because I love their product and I enjoy what they're doing and what they're about," he said.[11] It totally makes sense when you're a two-time World Series champion who has various companies approaching him for social media partnerships because of his 370,000-plus followers on Instagram. Hopefully other athletes will partner with brands they like to work with in the future and don't make it all about the money. When you post things on social media because of the money, the fans will notice that it's not authentic, and they won't engage with it.

I like to think of myself a very small cog in the history of sports social media. I've been a part of the top sports social media teams in the world. From Turner Sports to Bleacher Report to the NFL, I've had an inside look at what works and what doesn't work in sports social media. I've been a sponge that absorbed as much knowledge as possible wherever I've been. I've learned a lot along my eight-year career in the industry, but I need to constantly consume more information as platforms change and the consumption habits of the audience changes. You just got to roll with the punches in the sports social media world.

Just as Abernathy said, I don't know what the future holds, but I do know that the power of social media is in the hands of the audience. Wherever the audience decides to take the ever-changing industry of sports social media depends on them and them alone. The people in powerful places can't dictate how the audience should be spending their time and what content they should be consuming. That's what makes social media so special. Anyone can create an account, and they can follow, engage, and support whichever accounts they want. They have the freedom to do so. Sports social media accounts have a platform to post whatever they want, but fans have the right to choose what posts they want to engage with.

Be sure to keep an eye on original content, athlete content creation, and the increase of revenue in the future of sports social media. Those are three consistent themes that will play out in the years to come. The trends of the future might change, but every sports social media account needs to be ready for change and figure out ways to be a part of it and not fall behind. Change is uncertain. Natasha Bedingfield said in her song, "Today is where your book begins. The rest is still unwritten." I don't know where sports social media is headed in the future, but I do know I'm going to put my seatbelt on and enjoy the ride.

THE END

CITATIONS:

1. "Ralph Abernathy Quotes," Quote, Accessed February 18, 2021, https://quote.org/quote/i-dont-know-what-the-future-may-195894.

2. Troy Daniels, phone call with the author, January 22, 2021.

3. Dewayne Hankins, phone call with the author, January 15, 2021.

4. Randy Faehnrich, phone call with the author, December 28, 2020.

5. Blake Lawrence, phone call with the author, January 12, 2021.

6. Madilyn Zeegers, 2020, "How Much Does The Average NBA Player Make In His Career?" Sportscasting | Pure Sports, https://www.sports-casting.com/how-much-does-the-average-nba-player-make-in-his-career/.

7. Leslie Bloom, "How Long Is The Average Career Of An NFL Player?" Work - Chron, 2019, https://work.chron.com/long-average-career-nfl-player-12643.html.

8. Darren Heitner, "What Makes Juju Smith-Schuster A Social Media Sensation," Inc., 2017, https://www.inc.com/darren-heitner/what-makes-juju-smith-schuster-a-social-media-sensation.html.

9. Julie Burns, "How The Sports Industry Used The Rise Of Social Media," Industry Today, 2021, https://industrytoday.com/how-the-sports-industry-used-the-rise-of-social-media/.

10. Chris McGowan, Zoom call with the author, February 10, 2021.

11. Hunter Pence, phone call with the author, January 29, 2021.